Book 4

MAINLINE ENGLISH

T. F. Watson & G. H. Quinn

Illustrated by Angelo Cinque

 Holmes McDougall

© 1975 Holmes McDougall Ltd.

Printed & Published by Holmes McDougall Limited,
Allander House, 137–141 Leith Walk,
Edinburgh EH6 8NS

Designed by John Rushton Associates
Reproduced and Typeset by
Northern Book Reproductions, Beverley,
North Humberside

SBN: 7157 1361–2

Contents

* indicates Interpretation sections with a high proportion of additional language exercises.

MAKING SENTENCES

You can make a sentence about almost anything. You can say something about home, school, the street, friends, and so on.

Always remember that a sentence must make sense. It begins with a capital letter and ends with a full stop. Question sentences end with a question mark.

A Some of the following are good sentences, while others are not sentences at all. Write out the sentences:

1. The boy said he was
2. As I was leaving the school
3. As I was leaving the school I met my cousin.
4. When I reached the station
5. When I reached the station I found I had missed the train.
6. I shall wait here till Dad returns.
7. I shall not go out if
8. I shall not go out if it is wet.
9. How did the accident happen?
10. Is it true that

B Join the right parts to make good sentences:

1. The lifeboat was launched	on the runway
2. The accused man	in heavy seas
3. A traffic warden	by lightning
4. The crippled aeroplane landed safely	peals of thunder
5. The house was struck	directed the traffic
6. The lightning was followed by	was proved innocent

C Do the same here:

1. The soldier obeyed	while Mother watched TV
2. I will tell the truth	when he saw the policeman
3. Dad slept in the chair	until the storm died down
4. The man ran off	because it was his duty
5. I have lived in this house	if I am questioned
6. The ship remained in harbour	since I was a boy

D Use some of the words in the brackets to complete these sentences:

1. In our school we have . . .   (lessons, horses, games, concerts)
2. In our street there are . . .   (trains, buses, ships, houses)
3. At the circus there are . . .   (toys, clowns, elephants, plumbers)
4. At Christmas we receive . . .   (presents, blows, snow, visits)
5. On Saturday I like to . . .   (dance, play, snore, fly)
6. In the theatre we see . . .   (sports, plays, films, parades)
7. At the butcher's we bought . . .   (fish, meat, animals, toys)
8. For our holidays we went . . .   (outside, upstairs, abroad, far)

MAKING SENTENCES

A   Complete the following sentences in any way you please:
1. When the storm came on . . .
2. When the fireman arrived . . .
3. When the lady went into the shop . . .
4. When I leave school . . .
5. When we arrived at the station . . .
6. As we were watching TV . . .
7. As I looked out of the window . . .
8. As the players entered the field . . .
9. As the ship was leaving the harbour . . .
10. As I approached the house . . .

B
1. If you come with me . . .
2. If Sally had worked harder . . .
3. If Donald is late again . . .
4. If May comes to see me . . .
5. . . . if I had known the snow was so deep.
6. Although he was tired . . .
7. Although it was raining heavily . . .
8. Although poor . . .
9. . . . although I am only ten.
10. . . . although he was badly injured.

C   Five of the following sentences are true. The others are untrue. Which are the true ones?
1. Every sentence should begin with a capital letter.
2. A question sentence ends with a full stop.
3. A sentence should never make sense.
4. A courageous person is usually a coward.
5. An author writes books.
6. A vandal destroys or defaces property.
7. Christmas Day is on 25th July.
8. An ambitious man wants to get on well in the world.
9. Children are allowed to leave school at twelve years of age.
10. The proper names of people should begin with capital letters.

D   Complete these sentences:
1. While I was in town . . .
2. While I was listening to the radio . . .
3. While the party was going on . . .
4. I am not friendly with Hilary because . . .
5. I could not go out because . . .
6. Because I slept in . . .

JOINING SENTENCES - USING WHICH OR THAT

A   Make each pair of sentences into one sentence, using which **or** that:

Example 1.   I like the dress. Jean is wearing it.
I like the dress that Jean is wearing.

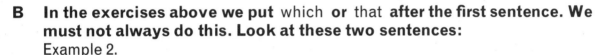

1.   The farmer has a bull. It has won many prizes.
2.   None of us believed the story. Sandra told it.
3.   We have a little dog. It barks nearly all day.
4.   Sheila deserved the prize. She won it.
5.   Someone has taken the coat. I left it in the cloakroom.
6.   I do not like the coat. Mother bought it for me.
7.   We tried to cross the stream. It flows past our house.
8.   Are you going to the circus? It is coming next week.

B   In the exercises above we put which **or** that **after the first sentence. We must not always do this. Look at these two sentences:**

Example 2.

The cake was burned in the **oven**. My mother baked **it**.

If we joined them as above the new sentence would be:

The cake was burned in the **oven which** my mother baked.

This is nonsense. My mother did not bake the oven.

The sentence should be:

The **cake**, **which** my mother baked, was burned in the oven.

You see we should always place which **or** that **as close as possible to the word to which it refers.**

Note how we use commas.

Now join these sentences in this way:

1.   The **picture** was painted by a famous artist. **It** hangs on the wall.
2.   The **house** was struck by lightning. **It** was occupied by my uncle.
3.   The **ship** drifted on to the rocks. **It** was wrecked.
4.   The flag was taken down. It had been flying at half mast.
5.   The house was struck by lightning. It was soon in flames.
6.   The ladder was not safe. The man was using it.
7.   The boat was built by my father. It sank in the storm.
8.   I sent my luggage by rail. It was very heavy.

C   Example 3

We found a **nest**. There were four eggs **in it**.
We found a **nest in which** were four eggs.

Now join the following sentences in this way:

1.   The **house** was an old one. I lived **in it**.
2.   Mother baked me a birthday **cake**. There were ten candles **on it**.
3.   This is the **book**. I was looking **for it**.
4.   I would like to see the **book**. John cut three pages from **it**.
5.   A vase stood on the table. There were eight red roses in it.

JOINING SENTENCES - USING WHO

A Example 1.

> I know the player. He scored the goal.
> I know the player who scored the goal.

Join the following sentences in this way:
1. This is the girl. She won the prize.
2. Here is the boy. He broke his leg.
3. I admire the girl. She is wearing the white dress.
4. The police soon captured the prisoner. He had escaped.
5. Here come the men. They are going to paint our house.

B **In the exercises above we put** who **after the first sentence. We must not always do this. Look at these two sentences:**
The thief was arrested by a policeman. He had broken into the shop.
If we joined them as we have already done, the sentence would be:
The thief was arrested by a policeman who had broken into the shop.
This, of course, is nonsense. It was not the policeman who had broken into the shop. It was the thief, so who **must be placed after** thief. **The joined sentence would then be:**
The thief, who had broken into the shop, was arrested by a policeman.

Now join these sentences:
1. The lady waved a flag. She was standing on the pavement.
2. The prisoner was soon captured. He had escaped.
3. The terrorists demanded a large ransom. They kidnapped the boy.
4. The hijackers threatened to blow it up. They seized the plane.
5. The lady wore a blue dress. She sat beside me.
6. The man fell off the ladder. He was cleaning our windows.
7. The boy is the cleverest in the class. He sits beside me.
8. The porter came from the West Indies. He carried my bags to the train.

USING WHOSE

C Example 1.

> This is the **boy. His father** is the pilot of an aeroplane.
> This is the boy whose father is the pilot of an aeroplane.

Example 2.

> I ran after the **lady**. I had found **her gloves** in the car.
> I ran after the lady whose gloves I had found in the car.

Now join these sentences. Put whose **as near as possible to the word to which it refers.**
1. I met a man. His home is in Edinburgh.
2. This is the little girl. Her doll was broken.
3. Dad met the **man**. We bought **his house**.
4. The **lady** has gone to the dentist. **Her teeth** have been causing her great pain.

5. The man complained to the police. His windows had been broken.
6. The sailors were taken off by helicopter. Their ship was wrecked.
7. The airmen were only slightly injured. Their plane crashed.
8. The lady was very grateful. I saved her dog from drowning.
9. The lady lives in the next street. We had looked after her cat.
10. The artist is a friend of mine. We admired his pictures.

D Example 3.

The **lady** was very distressed. The gems were stolen **from her house**.
The **lady, from whose house** the gems were stolen, was very distressed.
Now join these sentences in the same way:
1. The police arrested the **man**. The stolen goods were found **in his house**.
2. I met the **captain**. We sailed **in his ship**.
3. We met the **lady**. We used to live **in her house**.
4. I would like you to meet Mr Roberts. Dad used to work in his office.
5. The lady is very ill. We were going to her house this evening.
6. The man is very angry. We took the roses from his garden.
7. Dad met the officer. He served under his command during the war.
8. The lady is charming. We met the French officer in her house.

USING WHOM

Example 1.

That is the **man**. We met **him** a week ago.
That is the **man whom** we met a week ago.
Now join these sentences with whom:
1. I was speaking to the **lady**. We saw **her** in town.
2. We saw the **man**. The police arrested **him**.
3. This is the **boy**. I have invited **him** to the party.
4. The lady is very ill. You met her last week.
5. The girl is my sister. You gave her 50p.
6. The blind **man** thanked me. I helped **him** across the road.
7. The **lady** was very pleased. I had given my seat **to her**.
8. The lady admired my dress. I was speaking to her yesterday.
9. The soldier showed me his medal. I met him this morning.
10. The doctor attended to the old man. We had found him lying in the road.
11. Our friend has arrived. We were expecting him.
12. The **man** is my uncle. I went **with him** to the circus.

ALL SORTS

A People who come from **Wales** are **Welsh**. What do we call people who come from these countries?

England	Scotland	France	Spain	Italy
Denmark	Holland	Canada	Greece	China

B Join the right parts to make good sentences:

1. I nearly fainted — although we walked quickly.
2. Jean stayed in her bed — if I have sufficient money.
3. I put up my umbrella — when I saw the accident.
4. I will not speak to you again — because she was not feeling well.
5. We were late for school — when it began to rain.
6. I will buy the book — unless you apologise to me.

C Find the word that rhymes with:

1. **mole** — and means a baby horse.
2. **waste** — and means a part of one's body.
3. **tail** — and means a strong wind.
4. **mast** — and means quick.
5. **ground** — and means a hunting dog.
6. **rough** — and means not tender.
7. **love** — and means a pigeon.
8. **barrow** — and means not wide.
9. **sigh** — and means to weep.
10. **friend** — and means to repair.

D Improve the following sentences by changing the order of the words:

1. The blouse cost £5 which I bought.
2. The bag was found by a small boy which I lost.
3. The girl wore a white dress who sat beside me.
4. The taxi carried four people in which I travelled.
5. The pencil has a sharp point which I am using.
6. The roses have a lovely scent which grow in our garden.
7. The soldier was wounded in the war whom I met.
8. My uncle is now living with us whose house went on fire.

E Punctuate the following. The figure in the brackets tells you the number of sentences there should be in the passage.

1. my aunt motioned me to sit down I did so with my back to the window she asked me if I would like a cup of tea I declined (4)
2. at this point a man entered the room he looked a rather shifty character from the first moment i disliked him he did not look at me but addressed my aunt (4)
3. it was plain that my aunt did not trust him she listened attentively to what he had to say after a few minutes she rose and walked to the door she asked him to leave the house immediately (4)

WHO WILL BE THE HEIR?

A wise king had three sons. Wishing to find out which son was best fitted to succeed him, he asked them each this question:

"If you were to be a bird, which bird would you like to be?"

The first son replied, "I would like to be an eagle. He is a noble bird and the fiercest of all birds. With his great strength he rules them all."

The second son answered, "I would like to be a peacock, with fine, colourful feathers. I would be so handsome everybody would admire me."

The third son thought for a while and eventually said, "I would like to be an ordinary bird that flies with all the other birds. I would be friendly with them and would help them. In return they would, I am sure, help me."

When the shrewd old king was nearing his end, he chose one of his sons as his successor to the throne.

A

1. Why did the first son choose to be an eagle?
2. Was he a gentle person?
3. What did the second son admire about the peacock?
4. What do you think he took pride in?
5. Which son do you think the people would love and respect? Why do you think so?
6. Which of his sons do you think the king chose? Why?

B

1. **Some people are said to be 'as proud as a peacock'. Could you finish these comparisons by putting in the name of these birds?**

lark	owl	dove	hawk
as wise as an . . .	as swift as a . . .	as gentle as a . . .	as happy as a . . .

2. **Find the words in the passage which mean the following:**

suitable	follow	at last	good-looking	heir	wise

3. **Here are some words that can be used to describe birds:**

proud	plain	timid	fierce	tame
pretty	gentle	savage	beautiful	colourful

   Which ones would you use to describe the following?

an eagle	a peacock	a sparrow

ELEVEN DAYS ON A RAFT

This is a newspaper account of a seaman's miraculous escape from death.

A Brazilian seaman was recently admitted to a Liverpool hospital. He was in a very weak condition after spending eleven days in the Atlantic Ocean. Five of his shipmates had clung to a makeshift raft after their fishing boat sank off the coast of Guyana in South America. They existed on a ration of two mouthfuls of water a day.

As day followed day, the six survivors of a crew of fifteen became weaker and weaker.

One by one the helpless men lost their hold on the raft and slipped to their deaths. Eventually, only Inocencio was left but he, too, was too exhausted to hold on to the raft. He did not see the approach of a British ship travelling from Trinidad to Liverpool. Only when he woke up in hospital did he realise that he had managed to survive a terrible ordeal. Although almost completely exhausted, he was able to tell a Spanish-speaking nurse of his terrifying adventure.

A

1. Which language is spoken in Brazil?
2. What do you think happened to Inocencio's ship?
3. Why did the six seamen not lie on the raft?
4. How many of the crew were lost when the ship sank?
5. How many had lost their lives by the time Inocencio was rescued?
6. What kept the survivors alive while the raft was drifting?
7. For what country was the British ship bound?
8. Was Inocencio surprised to see it?
9. How do you think he felt when he woke up?
10. As he spoke only Spanish, how was he able to tell what had happened?

B

Imagine you are Inocencio. Tell in a few sentences the story of your miraculous escape.

DOG SAVES THREE IN HOUSE BLAZE

This headline appeared on the front page of a national newspaper. A young reporter witnessed the outbreak and questioned a number of people. This is his account of the incident which he sent to the news editor.

Eight Manchester families dressed in their nightclothes rushed from their flats in the early hours of this morning. A dog had given a fire alarm. Bruce, a two-year-old mongrel, whined and barked when the fire broke out in Janefield Street.

Bruce's howling awakened fourteen-year-old Elizabeth Smith. She was met by a 'wall of fire' in the kitchen. She quickly roused her young sister Mary and her mother, who had been ill for some weeks. Her father and her brother John were at a nearby factory where they were employed as cleaners.

Other families living in the block of flats were evacuated from their houses as firemen tackled the blaze. Their plan was to prevent the fire from spreading by sealing off the Smiths' flat.

A
1. How do you know this is a true story?
2. Who wrote the story?
3. How did he find out the actual facts?
4. Why did he send his account of what happened to the news editor?
5. When did the fire break out?
6. Why did the people not dress themselves before rushing out?
7. How was the alarm given?
8. Who was the first person to realise the danger?
9. Why were there no men in the flat at the time?
10. Why were the other families told to leave their flats?

B
1. Headline **is a compound word made up of** head **and** line. **See how many more compound words you can find in the passage.**
2. **Add another word to each of these words to make compound words:**

door	bed	wall	shop	stair	hose	arm	table

3. **Make nouns from these words:**

save	appear	young	give	meet	quick	ill
live	employ	clean	evacuate	prevent		

RESCUED BY ROPE

Near dawn, one Sunday morning, four climbers - three men and a young woman - were hauled by a rope to safety. They had been trapped on a narrow ledge near the summit of a mountain in the Cairngorms. They had huddled there, in lashing snow and sleet, for twelve hours on the ledge of a 250-feet sheer drop.

When darkness stranded the climbing party on the ledge two of the more experienced climbers began the dangerous descent. They managed to reach the bottom and gathered a party of volunteers to rescue their companions. As the rescue party struggled up the dark mountain the stranded climbers struck matches to guide them.

Early in the morning the shivering little group heard the first signalling whistle from the rescuers. Hot tea was lowered to them by a rope. By 5 a.m. the first of them was hauled up to an overhanging cliff. A man went first to test the rope. The girl followed and then the others.

About 5.30 a.m. five white rockets shot into the sky from the dark mountain peak. The people waiting at the foot of the mountain then realised that no one was seriously injured.

A
1. On what day did the party set out to climb the mountain?
2. How many climbers were in the party altogether?
3. What forced them to remain on the ledge?
4. Who were chosen to go for help and why?
5. Why were those on the ledge very uncomfortable?
6. How were the rescuers guided to the exact spot?
7. How did the stranded climbers first learn that help was near?
8. What was done to give them some strength?
9. How did the rescuers signal the result of the rescue?
10. What other signal might have been sent?

B
1. **What words in the passage mean the same as the following?**

daybreak	security	top	precipice	expert	perilous
way down	aid	try out	came after	lead	hurt

C Complete these sentences:
1. In mountain climbing ropes are used for . . .
2. The opposite of the word descent is . . .
3. People who are experienced have a lot of . . .
4. Volunteers are people who . . .
5. Climbers are sometimes stranded because . . .

ALI BABA AND THE FORTY THIEVES

Cassim and Ali Baba had shared equally in the small sum of money left by their father. Each then had been given the same chance of getting on in the world.

Cassim, however, married a rich wife and became, all at once, a wealthy merchant. Ali Baba, on the other hand, married a wife even poorer than himself. He lived in a hovel and earned a poor living by cutting wood in a forest and selling it in the Persian town where he lived.

One day, when Ali Baba had just finished loading his three asses, he saw a troop of horsemen galloping towards him. Fearing they might be robbers, he quickly climbed a tree which grew near a huge rock and hid amongst its thick branches. The horsemen dismounted beside the rock and removed their heavy saddle-bags. Then to Ali's astonishment, the captain cried out, "Open, Sesame!" Suddenly a door opened in the solid rock. After all the men had entered, the captain followed them and the door closed behind him.

A

1. **Here are a number of statements. Write down only those that are true:**
   (a) Ali and Cassim were brothers.
   (b) Their father was still alive.
   (c) Cassim's father was a rich man.
   (d) To begin with both had the same amount of money.
   (e) Cassim had received more than Ali.
   (f) It was only after years of hard work that Cassim became rich.
   (g) Ali lived in a fine house.
   (h) Ali's wife was a rich woman.
2. Was Ali's father a fair and just man? Give a reason for your answer.
3. In what country did Ali live?
4. How did he earn his living?
5. What was Ali doing when the horsemen appeared?
6. Why did he climb into the tree?
7. Why did the robbers fail to see Ali?
8. What, do you suppose, made the saddle-bags heavy?
9. How did the captain open the door?
10. Who was the last to enter the rock?

B

1. **What words in the passage mean the same as:**

opportunity	rich	enormous	ended	surprise
racing	all at once	got off	gone in	went after?

2. **Write down the opposites of these words:**

equally	small	same	rich	finish	heavy	quickly

3. **Complete these sentences using two of the words in each bracket:**
   (a) Cassim became very rich or .... He was not ... (wealthy, powerful, poor)
   (b) The captain was brave or .... He was not .... (cowardly, courageous, strong)
   (c) Robbers are dishonest or .... They are not .... (dangerous, honest, untrustworthy)
   (d) The horsemen were cunning or .... They were not .... (simple, crafty, clever)
   (e) Ali was cautious or .... He was not .... (timid, careful, reckless)

13

INVERTED COMMAS

Look at the picture.
It is quite clear what each boy is saying. The words actually spoken are placed inside balloons. Nothing else is in the balloons. Now, we have often to write down what people say. But we cannot always draw a picture and put the words spoken in balloons. Instead of balloons we put the words in inverted commas, like this:

" "

Notice it is only the first pair of commas that are inverted, or turned upside down.

A   Write these sentences and draw a ring round the words actually spoken, like this:

(a) I am going to the library said Joan.
    I'll go with you replied Linda.
    I want a book about wild birds explained Joan.

(b) I hope we are not going to be late remarked Sandra.
    We won't be late if you hurry up replied Sue.
    I can't walk quickly because I have a sore foot said Sandra.

B   Now, instead of drawing rings round the spoken words, put them in inverted commas, like this:

        "I am going to the library," said Joan.

Note that a comma is placed after the last word spoken, inside the inverted commas.
Write the sentences above, using inverted commas instead of rings.

C   Rewrite the following sentences, putting in inverted commas:

1.   I am going to London next week Ann boasted.
2.   I've been there many times Millie replied.
3.   We are going to visit Westminster Abbey Ann added.
4.   You should also go to the Tower said Millie.
5.   I believe it's a very interesting place answered Ann.

14

D **We may put the name of the person speaking at the beginning of the sentence, like this:**

> Gordon said, "I am going to see Jim."
> Donald replied, "Wait for me."

Note carefully:
(a) The first word spoken begins with a capital letter.
(b) A comma is placed before the inverted commas.
(c) The full stop at the end is inside the inverted commas.

Write the following sentences correctly:

> Jack said I am not going to wait any longer
> Jim replied wait for a few minutes
> Jack grumbled he is nearly always late
> Jim replied no he is usually in good time

E **If the words spoken ask a question, we put a question mark after the question, inside the inverted commas, like this:**
> "How many sums had you right?" asked the teacher.

Write the following sentences correctly:
(a) what is your name the teacher asked
(b) how old are you asked the policeman
(c) the teacher asked what is the capital of scotland
(d) is it edinburgh tommy replied
(e) Carol asked did you get your new dress

F **In the sentences we have already done, the words** not spoken **have been at the beginning or at the end of the sentence, like this:**
Ella said, "I am not going out because I have a cold."
The sentence can, however, be written in this way:
"I am not going out," said Ella, "because I have a cold."
Note carefully where the commas are used.

Punctuate fully these sentences:
1. Listen to me said the sailor and I will tell you a strange story.
2. I am enjoying myself said Marlene but I must go home soon.
3. I am certain remarked my father that there is no truth in her story.
4. Now whispered the old man I am going to show you something strange.
5. Perhaps you are right replied my mother but we had better make sure.
6. Move on said the policeman or you will find yourself in serious trouble
7. I cannot go remarked the boy because I have no shoes
8. We looked round the girl answered but we could see no one
9. What are you going to do when you leave school Bill asked.
10. I have no idea Jack replied.
11. Young man said my uncle we must be home before dark.
12. We will manage that without difficulty I answered.

NOUNS

A noun **is a naming word. So words like**
house, street, boy, chemist, grocer **are all nouns.**

A   Occupations
Pair these occupations with the correct descriptions:

A chemist	sells writing paper, pens and pencils.
A florist	drives a private motor car.
A stationer	sells medicines.
A chauffeur	writes stories for newspapers.
A mechanic	works with machines.
An optician	draws plans for buildings.
A journalist	sells flowers.
An architect	makes spectacles.

A man who performs operations is a	steeplejack
A person who makes cloth is a	surgeon
A man who repairs chimney stacks is a	author
A person who makes furniture is a	weaver
A man who loads and unloads ships is a	sculptor
A person who writes books is an	librarian
A person who works in a library is a	stevedore
A man who carves statues is a	cabinet maker

B   Homes

camp	monastery	convent	prison	igloo	palace

A nun lives in a . . . . .
Soldiers live in a . . . . .
An Eskimo's home is an . . . . .

A convict lives in a . . . . .
A monk lives in a . . . . .
A king lives in a . . . . .

C   Animals and their young
Pair these nouns correctly, like this: cat and kitten

Parent:	bird	frog	eagle	goose	dog	hen	lion
	goat	swan	sheep	horse	cow	duck	cat

Young:	lamb	kid	calf	foal	nestling	eaglet	pup
	kitten	gosling	cub	tadpole	duckling	chicken	cygnet

D   Sounds
Some nouns have been formed from the sound they make, like
the bang of a door   the screeching of brakes.

clatter	creak	crack	patter	popping	toot
dripping	crinkle	skirl	tinkle	rustling	hissing

Now choose the right word in the panel to complete the following:

the . . . of hoofs   the . . . of a whip   the . . . of water
the . . . of a hinge   the . . . of steam   the . . . of paper
the . . . of tiny feet   the . . . of corks   the . . . of leaves
the . . . of the bagpipes   the . . . of tiny bells   the . . of a horn

E

hangar	garage	prison	hospital	surgery
orchard	library	vineyard	reservoir	operating theatre

Choose from the list above the places where:

convicts are kept   books are kept
grapes are grown   sick people are looked after
fruit trees are grown   motor cars are kept
doctors consult their patients   aeroplanes are kept
operations are performed   water is stored

F   Form nouns from these verbs, e.g. grow - growth

admire	amuse	imitate	collect	confuse	arrive
laugh	enjoy	imagine	punish	prove	move
succeed	appear	encourage	choose	please	invite

G   Form nouns from these adjectives, e.g. strong - strength

long	broad	high	deep	cruel	strong
hot	free	sad	brave	weak	weary

H

arrival	appearance	victory	freedom	danger
love	guilt	courage	success	advantage
knowledge	entrance	abundance	loss	construction
enemies	hope	cleverness	purchase	patience

From the above list choose the words opposite in meaning to the words in italics.

A strange *disappearance*   To show a *profit*
The train's *departure*   The soldier's *cowardice*.
A great *defeat*   To live in *safety*
To live in *slavery*   A boy's *stupidity*
The *exit*   Our *allies* abroad
The prisoner's *innocence*   The *sale* of the house
The *destruction* of the bridge A great *hatred*
The man's *failure*   To his *disadvantage*
A feeling of *despair*   A *scarcity* of
To show *impatience*   To show *ignorance* of

M.E.4-B

ADJECTIVES

Adjectives are very useful words. They help us to describe a person or a thing in an interesting way. If they are carefully chosen we can see in our mind the person being described.

Try to see in your mind this old sailor:

He was a tall, strong, heavy man, with one leg. A tarry pigtail fell from the shoulders of his long, soiled, blue coat, and a black patch covered one eye.

He was a very silent man, yet not surly. His manner was curt but not offensive. His voice seemed cold and his attitude rude, but later I found him to be warm and polite. No one could accuse him of being dishonest, mean or cruel. His friends regarded him as the most upright, loyal and considerate of men.

A
1. Pick out all the adjectives in the description.
2. Give the opposites of as many of the adjectives as you can.
3. Which of these adjectives could you use to describe the appearance of one of your friends?

short	stout	plump	lean	slender	bent
stooped	fat	thin	dark	fair	tanned
strong	tall	ugly	neat	blue-eyed	attractive

B Which of these adjectives could you use to describe the nature or character of your Dad, your brother or sister, or some other person you know?

honest	dishonest	selfish	mean	quiet	noisy
polite	generous	impolite	mild	greedy	rude
gentle	affectionate	patient	haughty	insolent	loving
charming	good-natured	conceited	quick-tempered	loyal	demanding

1. Describe in two sentences the appearance of your teacher or your best friend.
2. Write two or three sentences about the nature of someone you know well.
3. Write two or three sentences about the old sailor.
4. From this list pick out three adjectives which have a similar meaning to each of the following:

(a) brave   (b) proud   (c) foolish   (d) dangerous

conceited	courageous	unwise	perilous	arrogant	risky
senseless	fearless	haughty	stupid	hazardous	daring

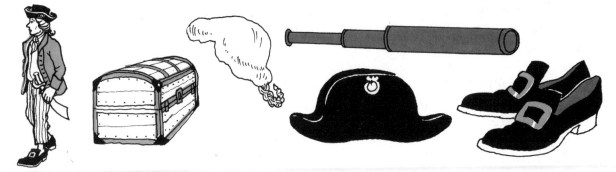

18

VERBS AND THEIR TENSES

The tense of a verb simply means the time when something happens. There are three simple Times or Tenses.

Present Tense tells of something that is happening now. Example: Each day the bus **leaves** on time.	Past Tense tells of something that happened in the past. Example: Yesterday the bus **left** on time.	Future Tense tells of something that will happen in the future. Example: Tomorrow the bus **will leave** on time.

A   Write out the following and fill in the missing sentences:

Present Tense	Past Tense	Future Tense
1. I run fast.	I ran fast.	I will run fast.
2. I see a red sky.	. . . .	. . . .
3. I come quickly.	. . . .	. . . .
4. I take my dinner.	. . . .	. . . .
5. I go to London.	. . . .	. . . .
6.	. . . .	The child will be good.
7.	Bob rose early.	. . . .
8.	. . . .	Sue will buy a coat.
9. Dad tells me a story.	. . . .	. . . .
10. My dog follows me.	. . . .	. . . .

B   Change all the present tenses to past tenses in the following sentences:
1.   The man is late for work because his watch is slow.
2.   The dog follows his master wherever he goes.
3.   I rise early every morning and go for a walk.
4.   I am very angry when I see him.
5.   I come home early and watch TV.
6.   Lena does her homework and then goes out to play.
7.   My uncle offers a reward to the person who finds his dog.
8.   As the soldiers march past the people cheer.
9.   On the table stands a vase which is filled with flowers.
10. When I come home I have a bath.

C   Change the verbs in this story to the present tense:
I heard a knock at the door. I opened it and looked out. There was no one there. I walked into the garden and saw a movement behind some bushes. I ran towards the bushes and found my best friend crouching there.

D   Change the verbs in these sentences to the future tense:
1.   I went to London.
2.   I gave the man money.
3.   He wrote a letter.
4.   She spoke to me angrily.
5.   The girl swam across the river.
6.   I ate all the sweets.
7.   I took his dinner.
8.   She bought a new coat.

PAST TENSES OF VERBS

Many people make bad mistakes when using the Simple Past Tense and the Past Tense with have, has, was, were, **etc.**
Study the following carefully. Go over them again and again until you are sure you can use them correctly.

Present Tense	Simple Past Tense	Past Tense with have
I see	I saw	I have seen
I go	I went	I have gone
I do	I did	I have done
I know	I knew	I have known
I take	I took	I have taken
I eat	I ate	I have eaten
I give	I gave	I have given
I bite	I bit	I have bitten
We speak	We spoke	We have spoken
We break	We broke	We have broken
We sing	We sang	We have sung
We swim	We swam	We have swum
We drink	We drank	We have drunk
We fall	We fell	We have fallen
We write	We wrote	We have written
We steal	We stole	We have stolen

A   Complete these sentences, using the correct word in the brackets:

1. I . . . the boy home.   We have . . . the boy home.   (taken, took)
2. John . . . the man.   Jim has . . . the man.   (saw, seen)
3. Bill . . . the work.   Jack has . . . the work.   (done, did)
4. I . . . my dinner.   Sue has . . . her dinner.   (ate, eaten)
5. Bill . . . home.   They have all . . . home.   (gone, went)
6. The dog . . . the child.   The child was . . . by the dog.   (bit, bitten)

B

1. Jack . . . the letter.   The letter was . . . by me.   (written, wrote)
2. Bob . . . the milk.   The milk was . . . by Sheila.   (drank, drunk)
3. Meg . . . my aunt.   I have . . . Jim for some time.   (knew, known)
4. Fred . . . the window.   Bill has . . . a window.   (broken, broke)
5. Joyce . . . a song.   Two songs were . . . by her.   (sang, sung)
6. I . . . to Sue.   I have . . . to the man.   (spoken, spoke)

C   Choose the correct words in the brackets to make good sentences:

1. When the ship (sunk, sank) we (swam, swum) for the shore.
2. Having (chose, chosen) the ring I (rang, rung) for my friend.
3. Most of the guests had (went, gone) before the last song was (sang, sung).
4. When the thief (saw, seen) the policeman, he (run, ran) away.
5. After we had (come, came), everyone (sit, sat) down for dinner.

ADVERBS

A **Words that go with verbs to tell something more about the action are called** adverbs. **They tell** when, where **or** how **something happened.**

> The boy ate his food **greedily**.   (How)
> My uncle visits us **weekly**.   (When)
> Jim waited **outside** for us.   (Where)

Below are ten adverbs, ending with ly. **Write them in a column and after each write its meaning:**

repeatedly	distinctly	causing death	stubbornly
politely	rapidly	on time	again and again
obstinately	punctually	at great speed	with good manners
accidentally	occasionally	all at once	not on purpose
fatally	suddenly	not very often	very clearly

B **Choose the most suitable of the above adverbs to complete these sentences.**

1. The boy . . . refused to tell the policeman his name.
2. The children were warned . . . not to go near the fire.
3. . . . there was a loud bang.
4. Our teacher always speaks . . .
5. The man was . . . injured in the car crash.
6. The two cyclists . . . collided with each other.
7. The fire spread . . . through the house.
8. We go . . . to the theatre.
9. Sally arrived . . . at the church.
10. The girl listened . . . to the lady.

C **Choose any five of the adverbs and use them in sentences of your own.**

D **Use these adverbs in the sentences below:**

> seldom   mistakenly   comfortably   greedily   always
> cheerfully   tomorrow   completely   loudly   patiently

1. Tom will be fit to go to school . . . .
2. We . . . go to the pictures.
3. The children waited . . . for their mother.
4. Dad was seated . . . in his favourite chair.
5. We cheered . . . when Don scored the winning goal.
6. Jack ate his supper . . .
7. Dad . . . locks the front door before going to bed.
8. I took the wrong book from the shelf . . .
9. The acquittal . . . vindicated the man's innocence.
10. We accepted the gloomy news as . . . as we could.

ALL SORTS

A   Join the right parts to make good sentences:

1. I spoke to the policeman
2. The police arrested the man
3. Tom scored the goal
4. Harry found the bag
5. Sally lost the umbrella
6. Quickly we ran up the stairs

who threw the bomb
who arrested the men
which led to the palace
which her father had given her
which won the match
which Sue had lost

B   Write the plurals of these nouns:

child	berry	mouse	cherry	knife	match
box	potato	monkey	office	jungle	woman

C   If these sentences are placed in their right order, they will tell a story:

It burst into flames.

They were badly hurt and were taken to hospital.

Fortunately a policeman managed to pull the two men to safety.

Yesterday a motor car was in collision with an oil tanker.

Fireman rushed to the scene but the car was completely burned out when they arrived.

D   Rewrite these sentences, putting in capital letters, inverted commas, commas and full stops:

1. manchester is a large city remarked donald
2. tom replied it is not nearly as large as london
3. I know that but it is very big all the same said donald
4. have you ever been to edinburgh asked ronnie it is a beautiful city

E   The following sentences are absurd. They do not make sense. What is wrong with them?

1. I don't like bananas but I do like fruit.
2. Sandra is much younger than she was ten years ago.
3. The match ended in a draw after John scored the winning goal.
4. Kate spent all her money and put the rest in the Savings Bank.
5. Uncle John is coming to see us last Saturday.
6. There were no vehicles in the street when the bus collided with the car.
7. My twin sister, Sheila, is a year older than I am.
8. Because it was so dark Mary had to switch off the light.
9. Most of the lies he told me were true.
10. It was raining because Mother was wearing her raincoat.

F   What nouns do we get from these verbs?

destroy	explode	invent	oppose	collect
confess	attract	imagine	govern	rebel
assist	appear	laugh	act	astonish

PREPOSITIONS

Look at the words in italics in these sentences:
1. Mother put the roses *in* a vase.
2. She put a mat *under* the vase.
3. She placed the vase *on* the table.
4. We watched her *with* interest.

These words are called prepositions and are always placed before a noun.

A   Here are some prepositions often used:

for	from	in	into	before	under	below	with
of	off	on	over	through	between	after	round

Choose the most suitable prepositions to complete these sentences:
1. Mother sent me . . . the shop.
2. She sent me . . . butter.
3. Sheila came . . . me.
4. Jim dived . . . the water.
5. I took the money . . . the child.
6. The train left . . . time.
7. We shared the money . . . us.
8. The vase fell . . . the table.
9. We walked . . . the field.
10. We sheltered . . . a tree.

B   Write sentences, each containing one of the prepositions above.

C   Here are some phrases beginning with a preposition:

in the drawer	through the snow	above the clouds
in terror	for his kindness	along the street

Now choose the most suitable phrase to complete these sentences:
1. We trudged . . . .
2. The animals fled . . . from the fire.
3. Mother put her purse . . .
4. We thanked the gentleman . . . to us.
5. The jet plane flew high . . . .
6. The frightened horse bolted . . . .

D

on his departure	in the hope of seeing	in pursuit of
with great vigour	in the darkness	without a moment's hesitation
in the act of	in abundance	in the neighbourhood
at the thought of	for his cruelty	in a fit of temper

Replace the words in heavy type with the most suitable phrases from the list above:
1. The thief was caught **while he was** stealing the gems.
2. The travellers lost their way **because it was dark**.
3. We were friendly with the people who lived **round about**.
4. Jack trembled **on thinking** of the danger he had just escaped.
5. We stood in front of the palace **because we hoped to see** the Queen.
6. The giant was hated **because he was so cruel**.
7. Crowds cheered the President **when he was going away**.
8. The bloodhounds set off **after** the escaped convict.
9. **As quickly as he could** Jim dived into the water.
10. Apples are in the shops **in great numbers**.
11. They rowed the boat **as hard as they could**.
12. Donald rushed from the room **very angrily**.

23

PUNKIES

Punkie is a name for a mangold or turnip which has been hollowed out. Faces or designs are carved on the outside, and a lighted candle placed inside. In the darkness there appears a startling, lit-up face. The effect can be quite frightening.

An old legend tells that the men of a village in Somerset lost their way home from a fair. The night was foggy, and they wandered into a field of turnips. One produced a candle, hollowed out a turnip with his knife, and thus cleverly invented a lantern. Meanwhile the women went out hunting for the men, wearing scarlet cloaks. Soon a custom developed. Now many places have an annual event, and prizes are awarded for the best punkie. Sometimes the children decorate their punkies with colourful designs and go round in a procession chanting

"It's punkie night to-night,
It's punkie night to-night.
Give us a candle, give us a light,
It's punkie night to-night".

Some people observe this old custom at Hallowe'en or Holy Evening, the evening before the church festival of All Saints. An old belief is that the lights and the chanting keep away the evil spirits. Perhaps that is why we see pictures of witches flying about on broomsticks.

A

1. What is a punkie?
2. Why do people make punkies?
3. When can they cause alarm?
4. What kind of story is a legend?
5. What is an invention?
6. What is a custom?
7. How did punkie-making become a regular custom?
8. What effect did chanting have according to some people?
9. Why would you call these people superstitious?

B

1. (a) A person who invents is an ...   He makes ...
   (b) A person who decorates is a ...   He makes ...
   (c) A person who observes is a ...   He makes ...

2. **What words in the passage mean the following?**

pattern	cut out	very surprising	result	brought out	once a year

3. **Find out about Christmas, New Year and Easter customs.**

THE MILLION BUS TICKET RUMOUR

"I hear that all children must attend school seven days a week," declared Bertie.

"That's only a rumour that's going around," said Bill.

" What's a rumour?" inquired Bertie.

Bill replied, "It's a story that someone made up. It spreads and spreads and becomes stranger and stranger. Everybody that hears it adds something to it."

Dad was smiling to himself. "When I was a boy," he said, "I tried to collect a million bus tickets."

"What use are a million used bus tickets?" asked Bertie.

"No use at all, unfortunately," sighed Dad. "The story went round that you could exchange them for a Rolls Royce car. I collected two hundred and thirty six and then gave up."

"Did anyone win a Rolls Royce?" asked Bill.

"What do you think?" replied Dad. "Joe Brown thought he could exchange a million bus tickets for an invalid chair. Joe was always trying to help people. Jack Jones was after a guide dog for the blind. Dick Dean set his heart on a racing yacht. No one really wanted their bus tickets, and no one ever knew how the rumours started."

Mum came in with scrambled eggs and toast for supper. "I hear, Edward, that you and the boys are going to wash up," she said hopefully.

Dad looked slyly at his sons and laughed, "That's only a rumour."

A
1. How does a rumour start?
2. What happens to it later?
3. Why did Dad try to collect so many bus tickets?
4. Why did he give up his attempt?
5. Why did Joe Brown want an invalid chair?
6. What makes you think he and Jack Jones were unselfish?
7. Was Dick Dean just as unselfish?
8. What was Dad's excuse for avoiding washing up?

B Complete these sentences about rumours:
1. There is a rumour that . . . for a Rolls Royce car.
2. It is silly to believe this because . . . .
3. Rumours start when . . . .
4. A lovely rumour is going around our school that . . . .
5. I do not believe this rumour because . . . .

DANNY MURPHY

He was as old as old could be,
His little eye could scarcely see,
His mouth was sunken in between
His nose and chin, and he was lean
And twisted up and withered quite,
So that he couldn't walk aright.

His pipe was always going out,
And then he'd have to search about
In all his pockets, and he'd mow
"O, deary me!" "musha now!"
And then he'd light his pipe, and then
He'd let it go clean out again.

He couldn't dance or jump or run,
Or ever have a bit of fun
Like me and Susan, when we shout
And jump and throw ourselves about:
- But when he laughed, then you could see
He was as young as young could be!

James Stephens

A
1. Which country do you think Danny came from?
2. Why did Danny have difficulty in walking?
3. Which of these things wither with age: oak tree, car, street, rose, plant?
4. What makes you think Danny was forgetful?
5. Why do you think his memory was poor?
6. What unusual word in the poem do you think means *mutter*?
7. Give three reasons why Danny couldn't have fun.
8. What makes you think Danny was young in heart although old in years?

B
1. **Which of these adjectives could you use to describe Danny?**

deaf	dumb	lame	frail	stooped	lazy
light-hearted		half-blind		good-humoured	
elderly	idle	agile	weary		

2. **Complete these sentences:**
   (a) Although he was elderly, Danny . . . .
   (b) When he wanted to smoke, Danny . . . .
   (c) Because of . . ., Danny could not dance or run.
   (d) Danny often had to search his pockets for . . . .

THE SAUCY SAILOR

"Come, my own one; come, my fond one,
  Come, my dearest, unto me.
Will you wed with a poor sailor lad
  Who has just returned from sea?"

"O indeed, I'll have no sailor,
  For he's dirty, smells of tar.
You are ragged, you are saucy -
  Get you gone, you Jacky Tar!"

"If I'm dirty, if I'm ragged,
  If, maybe, of tar I smell,
Yet I've silver in my pocket
  And a store of gold as well!"

"Indeed, sir, I was joking -
  I am quite beneath your spell.
Ragged, dirty, tarry sailors
  I love more than words can tell."

"Do you take me to be foolish,
  Do you think that I am mad? -
That I'd wed the like of you, miss,
  When there's others to be had?

"No, I'll cross the briny ocean,
  No, my boat shall spread her wing.
You refused me, ragged, dirty -
  Not for you the wedding ring!"

English folk-song

A
1. Who opens the conversation in this poem?
2. To whom did he make a proposal?
3. What offer did he make?
4. How was his proposal received?
5. What reasons did she give for refusing?
6. What made her later change her mind?
7. Why did she say she had been joking?
8. What made the young man change his mind?
9. How do you think the young lady felt about this?
10. Do you think the sailor was right in deciding not to marry her? Why?

B   What do these words in the poem mean?
1. Saucy means . . .   fond of sauce, cheeky, wealthy.
2. Jack Tar is a . . .   man who tars roads, tar merchant, sailor.
3. Spell means a . . .   charm, short period of time, correct word.
4. Briny means . . .   calm, stormy, salty.
5. The boat's wing is the . . . steering wheel, bow, sails.

C   Pair each noun with the most suitable adjective:

generous	correct	blunt	foolish	conceited	angry
refusal	joke	offer	discussion	decision	girl

D   Pair each verb with the most suitable adverb:

punctually	limply	greedily	stealthily	quickly	loudly
eat	creep	read	snore	walk	arrive

A GALLOP ON THE MOTORWAY

This is a newspaper report of an incident on the M74 motorway near Hamilton, in Scotland.

Mercat, a Yorkshire racehorse, had been entered for the 3.45 race at Hamilton Race Course. During a practice canter he threw his jockey. He galloped out of the racecourse down the M74 motorway, breaking every rule in The Highway Code. If he had been a motorist, he would have been charged with the following offences:

    going through traffic lights at red;
    going the wrong way, to the right, on a roundabout; and,
    proceeding in a dangerous manner.

Mercat, at least, did not exceed the speed limit. A motorway policeman received an S.O.S. on his radio: "Proceed North to Hamilton and look out for a runaway racehorse!"

"What next!" thought the constable. Driving along the motorway, he passed a line of slow-moving cars. There at the head of the procession was Mercat! The constable sprang out of his car and placed himself in front of the surprised and terrified horse. He put up his hand and said softly, "Come here, boy." Mercat obediently trotted over to him. At that moment a car drew up. The driver turned out to be a member of the Glasgow Mounted Police and he rode Mercat back to the racecourse. Mercat was none the worse for his adventure. He came in second in the 3.45 race.

A Only seven of the following sentences are true. Write them out.

1. This is an imaginary story.
2. It is a true incident reported in a newspaper.
3. Mercat bolted when taking part in the race.
4. Mercat bolted before the race began.
5. Motorists could travel at any speed on the motorway.
6. It was against the law to exceed the speed limit.
7. A motorway policeman was ordered to look out for a runaway horse.
8. He saw the horse at the head of a slow-moving procession of cars.
9. When he called the horse to him, it obeyed.
10. A passing motorist rode the horse back to the racecourse.
11. Mercat ran in the race and won it.

B

1. In what ways are motorways different from ordinary roads?
2. Which of these are not allowed on motorways?

pedestrians	bicycles	horses
vans	coaches	scooters

3. Why was Mercat's gallop reported in the newspaper?
4. What is a practice canter?
5. In what ways was Mercat a danger to motorists?
6. Why were the cars proceeding very slowly?
7. How do you think the motorists felt?
8. How did the policeman learn about the runaway horse?
9. Why do you think Mercat trotted over quietly to the policeman?
10. What is (a) The Highway Code? (b) An S.O.S.?

C The word **motorway** is made up of two different words, **motor** and **way**. Such a word is called a compound word (or double word).

How many other compound words can you find in the story?

D The expression **turned out to be** near the end of the story means **was found to be.** Here are some expressions containing the word **turn**. Pair them with their correct meaning:

1. to turn down
2. at every turn
3. to turn up
4. to a turn
5. to turn one's stomach
6. to do someone a good turn
7. to have a good turn of speed
8. to turn tail
9. in turn
10. about turn

to help someone in some way
perfectly
in the correct order
to make one sick
to be able to go very fast
to change one's mind
at every opportunity
to appear or happen
to go right round
to reject

29

CHOOSING WORDS

A **Choose the most suitable of these** nouns **to complete the sentences below:**

leaves	lights	thunder	paper	birthday	bicycle
fence	trees	houses	handle	door	warmth
car	sun	policeman	spectacles	lightning	

1. The . . . were falling and the . . . were almost bare.
2. The . . . turned red and he had to stop his . . . suddenly.
3. Mother couldn't read the . . . without her . . . .
4. The . . . was loud and the . . . flashed.
5. On her . . . Sandra received a . . . .
6. A . . . separates the two . . . .
7. A . . . saw a man turning the . . . of the . . . .
8. The young lady enjoyed the . . . of the . . . .

B **Do the same with these** adjectives:

frisky	hungry	delicious	sleepy	rusty	blazing
busy	dense	poisoned	proud	burning	frightened
cosy	clever	green	large		

1. The . . . lambs chased each other in the . . . meadow.
2. The food looked . . . but I was not . . . .
3. Dad felt . . . before the . . . fire.
4. The . . . horse bolted along the . . . street.
5. Clouds of . . . smoke rose from the . . . ship.
6. The old woman sat in a . . . corner of the . . . room.
7. The nail was . . . and gave him a . . . finger.
8. The . . . parent watched her . . . child receive his prize.

C **Choose a suitable** noun **and an** adjective **from this list to complete the sentences below:**

climbers	rocks	man	hospital	goals
victory	sea	jungle	result	beautiful
narrow	guilty	hunting	injured	strong
wrecked	famous	visiting	fashion	

1. The . . . crept along the . . . ledge.
2. The . . . ship drifted on to the jagged . . .
3. The . . . man was taken to . . .
4. The . . . team scored four . . .
5. The . . . man fainted on hearing the . . . of the trial.
6. Lord Nelson won a . . . . at Trafalgar.
7. The . . . party set off into the . . .
8. A . . . breeze blew in from the . . .
9. The . . . girl was a . . . model.

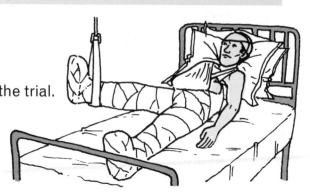

30

PUNCTUATION

Read this passage:

the woman heard a loud piercing scream at once she left her car and looked around she could see nothing it was too foggy had that terrible cry come from a human being or from an animal she did not know but she had to find out.

Perhaps you had difficulty in making any sense out of the passage, because there are no capital letters and no full stops. There is nothing to show where one sentence ends and another sentence begins.

Now look at the difference when it is properly punctuated:

The woman heard a loud, piercing scream. At once she left her car and looked around. She could see nothing. It was too foggy. Had that terrible cry come from a human being or from an animal? She did not know but she had to find out.

The following passages complete the story, but they are not punctuated. Punctuate them properly. The figure in the brackets tells you the number of sentences there should be in the passage.

1. she took a torchlight from a pocket in the car there was a wood nearby had that cry come from there (3)

2. she was not afraid she called out but there was no answer pulling her coat more closely round her she entered the wood (3)

3. she flashed her torch she called out again not a sound was to be heard in the stillness of the night (3)

4. after a time she decided to return to her car she was just about to start up the engine when she heard another terrible cry for the first time she began to feel afraid she sat motionless and listened (4)

5. after a few minutes she drove off when she reached the village she went to the police station she told the sergeant at the desk what had happened he said they would investigate without delay (4)

6. with torchlights in their hands two policemen went into the wood by this time the fog was becoming thicker they searched everywhere but could find nothing it was useless to search any further (4)

7. next morning they went back to search again the fog had almost cleared after half-an-hour they found a scarf and nearby a man's hat soon they found an injured man lying unconscious in the grass (4)

8. an ambulance soon arrived and the injured man was rushed to hospital he was found to have a severe wound in his head a policeman sat by his bedside he would wait until the man was able to talk and tell what had happened the surgeon told him that this might be some time the policeman did not mind (6)

THE APOSTROPHE

A raised comma (') called an apostrophe is used to show that something belongs to a person.

For example, if we are talking about the dress belonging to Mary, we write Mary's dress. We put an apostrophe after Mary and add the letter s. Similarly Helen's shoes means the shoes belonging to Helen, and the fisherman's nets means the nets of the fisherman.

Write the following in this short way:

1. The car belonging to Dad.
2. The shop owned by my uncle.
3. The pencil belonging to Tom.
4. The money belonging to Sue.
5. The dog belonging to the shepherd.
6. The cats of our neighbour.

Write the following, putting in the apostrophe:

Jims bag	Jeans coat	Freds cap	Jacks house
a dogs collar	Dads army	a cats tail	a childs doll

Look carefully at this sentence:

The **birds'** nests were blown down by the wind.

Birds is a plural word and so only an apostrophe is used. In this case we do not add s.

Write the following in this way:

the cages for the lions
the stables for the horses
the hoofs of the horses

the nests of the birds
the room used by the teachers
the roofs of the houses

Look at this sentence: The **men's** cloakroom is closed.

Men is a plural word and yet we have added an apostrophe and the letter s.

The rule is: If the plural word does not end with s, we add both an apostrophe and the letter s, like this:

the children's party   the women's coats   the geese's feet

ANOTHER USE OF THE APOSTROPHE

The apostrophe is used to show that two words have been joined together to make one word.

For example, we say I'm for I am, he's for he is, isn't for is not.

Note carefully that the apostrophe is placed where a letter or letters have been missed out. This is important.

Now write the following in this short way:

we are	we have	they have	I have
you are	they are	do not	will not
do not	can not	would not	must not

Rewrite the following sentences, putting in apostrophes where necessary:

1. Ive told her she mustnt be late.
2. Ive found my bag, but Sheila cant find hers.
3. Well go if youll go.
4. I mustnt go to the party because Ive a bad cold.
5. Wheres the dogs collar. I dont know.
6. "Whos for tennis?"

USING A DICTIONARY

In a dictionary words are arranged in alphabetical order, and in a telephone directory names are also arranged in alphabetical order. Why? Think how difficult it would be to find words if they were not arranged in this way.

A Arrange these letters in **ABC** or alphabetical order:

1. c a t d o g h i l b
2. y z k a l e n q p r
3. c t l b s d f m o h

Arrange the following words in alphabetical order:

4. dog   cat   kitten   wolf   hen   lion
5. fire   ass   carpet   light   pen   bath
6. Jane   Bill   Carol   Ethel   Ann   Enid
7. York   Dover   Perth   Bury   Hull   Aberdeen

B Look at these words:

          attic   apple   after   ass   about

These five words all begin with the same letter a. To arrange them in alphabetical order we look at the second letter.
Arranged in alphabetical order the second letters are:

          b   f   p   s   t

So the words are:

          about   after   apple   ass   attic

Now arrange the following words in this way:

1. desk   duck   dock   date   din
2. fun   fire   fell   fate   foot
3. bill   bath   book   but   bell
4. come   cent   crook   car   cheek
5. grass   ghost   gem   gas   glen

C If the first two letters are the same we look at the third letter.

          cape   cart   cattle   can   cabin

Arranged in alphabetical order the third letters are:

          b   n   p   r   t

So the words in alphabetical order are:

          cabin   can   cape   cart   cattle

D Write these words in a column. Use your dictionary to find the meaning of each word and write it after the word:

amazement	frightful	sturdy	honest
ample	frightening	stray	mangle
bashful	fearsome	scowl	jaw
burly	honourable	repulse	report
donation	jetty	prompt	mingle

M.E.4-C

AND **OR** BUT

Look at these sentences:

Mother went into the dress shop.
She bought a beautiful new dress.

They may be joined in this way:

Mother went into the dress shop **and** bought a beautiful new dress.

We use and **to join the sentences because Mother did what she might have been expected to do in a dress shop.**

Now look at these sentences:

Mother went into the dress shop.
She bought nothing.

They are joined in this way:

Mother went into the dress shop **but** bought nothing.

In this case we join the sentences with but **because something unexpected followed.**

A   Now join these sentences, using and **or** but:
1.   I went to the football match. I found it very exciting.
2.   I went to the football match. I did not find it exciting.
3.   I knocked at the door. No one answered it.
4.   My aunt gave me a present. I thanked her for her kindness.
5.   I bought a pair of shoes. They did not fit me.
6.   The man dived into the river. He rescued the boy.
7.   I offered the man a good price for the car. He would not sell it.
8.   Jack gave me an orange. I did not like it.

Now look at these sentences:

I saw the thief coming out of the house.
I ran after him.
I did not catch him.

They can be joined to make one sentence, like this:
I saw the thief coming out of the house **and** ran after him, **but** I could not catch him.
Notice that the word I **in front of** ran **has been left out.**

B   Join the following sentences, using both and **and** but:
1.   I opened the door. I looked out. I could see no one.
2.   I went to the bus stop. I waited for ten minutes. Sue did not turn up.
3.   The men grasped the rope. They pulled with might and main. They could not move the huge tree.
4.   We put on our coats. We went out. We could not find the dog.
5.   The hunter took careful aim. He fired. He missed the tiger.
6.   The boy fell off the tree. He hurt his leg. He was able to walk home.
7.   Bill bought a puppy. He took it home. His Dad would not let him keep it.
8.   I went into the shop. I asked the price of a coat. I thought it was too dear.

34

ALL SORTS

A Join each group of sentences into one good sentence. Use words such as and, who, which, as, when, **etc.**

1. The hunter took careful aim. He fired at the tiger's head.
2. We came across a number of natives. They were working in the fields.
3. I lay in bed. I heard someone. He was walking up the garden path.
4. I heard a cry. I dived into the water. I swam towards the boy.
5. The girl reached the side of the river. She put the basket in the water. She watched it float away.
6. I felt extremely tired. I lay down on the grass. I slept for several hours.
7. I looked from my window. I saw a car. It was travelling at great speed.
8. We hurried upstairs. We found the children. They were hiding in a corner of the room.

B Join the right ending to the beginning of each sentence:

1. Dad warned us
2. The shepherd informed us that
3. The prisoner protested that
4. The policeman told us that
5. I advised John
6. The firemen declared that

our house had been burgled.
they could not save the house.
to go home at once.
not to go near the pond.
he had lost five sheep in the storm.
he was innocent.

C Complete these sentences in any way you please:

1. Mother thinks that . . .
2. We now know that . . .
3. I believe that . . .
4. I told our teacher that . . .
5. The motorist admitted that . . .
6. The boy said that . . .

D Arrange the words in each line in alphabetical order:

1. agony   abroad   arch   answer   avenue   adverb
2. clock   choice   cable   cushion   cruet   cell
3. dive   dust   date   drop   deer   double
4. plot   party   peach   profit   punch   pitch
5. sort   serve   satin   surf   sink   speck
6. trip   trek   tramp   trust   trail   trot

E Rewrite the following sentences correctly:

1. where did you put my bag joe asked.
2. youll find it in the bedroom my mother answered.
3. its not there replied joe.
4. look properly and youll find it snapped my mother.
5. Ive looked but I cant see it grumbled joe.

F Match these verbs and adverbs:

| Verbs: | explain | listen | charge | creep | fall |
| | shine | shiver | chatter | breathe | wait |

| Adverbs: | cautiously | patiently | carefully | brightly | incessantly |
| | heavily | furiously | fearfully | deeply | attentively |

BEATEN TO THE POST

James Chalmers was a man of many ideas. Perhaps he learned a lot from the books he sold. He was a bookseller in Dundee more than a hundred years ago. James turned his inventive mind to the problem of sending letters cheaply and efficiently. At that time there were no postage stamps. The person receiving a letter had to pay for it according to the distance the letter had travelled.

James Chalmers considered the possibility of making the sender of the letter pay. This could be done in various ways. The simple idea of attaching a paper sticker on the letter occurred to James. The sticker could have some mark placed on it by the person in charge of the post. The recipient would have no charge to pay. To impress the Government with his idea he designed some small paper stickers, with different prices marked on them.

The Postmaster General, the famous Rowland Hill, was most impressed by this simple suggestion. He had some stickers made in black and white and marked 'one penny', and others in red and white marked 'two pence'. The Queen's head was stamped on them. In this way the first postage stamps were issued to the public. Rowland Hill became world famous as the inventor of the postage stamp. James Chalmers has been forgotten.

A
1. What is the meaning of "beaten to the post" in this story?
2. What does, "Mercat the racehorse was beaten to the post" mean?
3. How many ways can you think of for sending letters?
4. Sometimes "carrier" pigeons carry messages. How many reasons can you think of for this being inefficient?
5. Is it cheaper to send a letter from Edinburgh to London than from Oxford to London?
6. In what ways are modern postage stamps different from "paper stickers"?
7. What did Rowland Hill think of the idea that James Chalmers offered?
8. Why do you think James Chalmers did not become famous?
9. How was he "beaten to the post"?
10. Who was Queen during this period?

B Complete these sentences:
1. Inventors are people who . . .
2. Postage stamps are used . . .
3. A recipient is a person who . . .
4. James Chalmers' simple idea made a great . . . on Rowland Hill.

THE GERFALCON

One of Scotland's rarest visitors, a white gerfalcon, flew in recently.

However, he did not fly in under his own wing power. The falcon travelled in style to Aberdeen airport by helicopter.

Two days ago the falcon, whose natural home is in Greenland or the Canadian Arctic, landed exhausted on the oil rig 'Ocean Rover', almost 140 miles off Aberdeen.

The crew thought he was an osprey, and fed him five pounds of trout while he was waiting for his flight to the mainland.

It was not until he arrived in Aberdeen that zoo manager George Leslie and head keeper John Buchan identified him.

Underwater engineer Bob Baxter, 24, from Ellon, Aberdeenshire, who helped to trap the falcon on the rig, returned on the same flight.

He said: "The bird was exhausted when he landed on the rig, and we had no trouble catching him. He was herded into the television room, then we turned a cardboard box on its side and he just walked into it."

Mr Leslie said: "The bird is still exhausted, but we will take him to the zoo and nurse him back to health, then release him in Orkney or Shetland."

A **Read the passage carefully and then complete the sentences below in your own words:**

1. People in our country are surprised to see gerfalcons because . . .
2. The gerfalcon travelled to Aberdeen by helicopter because . . .
3. He landed on the oil rig after . . .
4. He flew such a distance that . . .
5. Thinking he was an osprey, the crew . . .
6. The oil rig crew fed him just before . . .
7. No one knew what kind of bird he was until . . .
8. The crew had no difficulty in catching him because . . .
9. The gerfalcon was trapped when . . .
10. Until . . . he will be kept at the Zoo.

B Airport **is a compound word made up of** air **and** port. **Find three other compound words in the story.**

C **Pair words on the top and bottom lines to form compound words:**

make	fly	thunder	loose	air	black
storm	bird	craft	shift	leaf	paper

SHIPWRECKED IN THE SOUTH SEAS

For many months we lived quite happily on our lonely island. Sometimes we went fishing, other times we went hunting in the woods, or climbed to a mountain top in the hope of seeing a vessel which we might hail.

One day Jack and I were sitting on the rocks, and Peterkin was wringing the water from his clothes, having fallen by accident into the sea. Suddenly I saw two objects on the horizon.

"What are they?" I asked Jack.

"I can't imagine," he answered, "I've noticed them for some time and thought they were black seagulls."

"They seem to be coming towards us," I said.

"Hello! What's wrong?" inquired Peterkin.

"Look there!" cried Jack.

"Whales!" cried Peterkin, shading his eyes with his hand. "No - can they be boats, Ralph?"

Our hearts beat with excitement at the very thought of seeing human faces again. I noticed, however, a worried look on Jack's face. At last he said, "They are canoes. We must hide, for no doubt the men in them are cannibals. I have heard that the natives of these South Sea Islands are all cannibals."

A

1. Name the three persons in the passage.
2. Which one is telling the story?
3. How did the boys spend their time on the island?
4. What special reason did they have for climbing the mountain?
5. Why did the objects at first seem so small?
6. What were they first mistaken for?
7. What did Peterkin think they were?
8. Why were the boys so excited?
9. Where do you think the men in the canoes came from?
10. What reason was there to fear the natives of the South Sea Islands?

B

1. **Complete these sentences using** -ing:
   (a) The boys went fish. . . in the sea.
   (b) They liked swim. . . and div. . .

2. **Now write your own sentences using words ending with** -ing.

come	drive	strike	ski	fly
bake	dance	live	shove	face

3. **Complete these sentences using** -ed, -d or -en:
   (a) Peterkin has fall. . . in the sea.
   (b) Jack has hear . . . a ship.

4. **Now write sentences using** has **or** have **and these words:**

tried	spied	seen	eaten
wrung	done	drunk	said
flown	crept	gone	thought

C Find out:

1. The names of some of the South Sea Islands.
2. What you would need to survive on a desert island.
3. What you would be able to make from wood.

THE CAPTAIN

My father kept the 'Admiral Benbow' Inn. One day a brown old seaman, with a sword-cut across one cheek, came and took lodging under our roof. He was a tall, strong, heavy man, with a tarry pigtail falling over the shoulders of his soiled blue coat. Bad as his clothes were, and coarsely as he spoke, he had none of the appearance of a man who had sailed before the mast. He seemed more like the mate or skipper, accustomed to being obeyed.

We were told that the stage-coach had set him down the morning before at the 'Royal George' Inn. He had inquired what inns there were along the coast and had chosen to stay in ours. It was well spoken of and was described as isolated.

He was a very silent man by custom. All day he hung round the cove, or upon the cliffs, with a brass telescope. All evening he sat in a corner of the parlour next to the fire. Mostly he would not speak when spoken to, but look up angrily and blow his nose like a fog-horn. We and the people who came to our house soon learned to let him be.

A 1. Give the names of the two inns mentioned in the passage.
2. Why did the sea captain want to stay at an inn?
3. Give two reasons why he preferred the 'Admiral Benbow'.
4. What do you think had happened to his cheek?
5. How do you know that the people in the story lived a long time ago?
6. How did the captain usually spend the day?
7. How did he usually spend his evenings?
8. How did he act when people spoke to him?

B 1. **Make nouns from these words:**

strong	carry	coarse	speak	sail	obey
inquire	describe	chose	silent	angrily	

2. **Complete these sentences:**
   (a) My father was the . . . of the 'Admiral Benbow'.
   (b) The captain became a . . . in our inn.
   (c) The captain's speech was very . . .
   (d) A . . . is in charge of a ship.
   (e) A . . . was once used to carry passengers.
   (f) A . . . is used for seeing things in the distance.

3. **Complete the second sentence, using one of the three adjectives in the brackets.**
   (a) Tom handed in the purse he found. He was . . . (selfish, honest, careful).
   (b) Eddie never shared his sweets. He was . . . (generous, hasty, selfish).
   (c) John is not afraid of bullies. He is very . . . (brave, cowardly, loyal).
   (d) Doreen never wastes time. She is very . . . (good-natured, hard-working, slow).

BOTTLE HILL - An Irish Legend

Mick Mulligan had a poor farm in Ireland in a place called Mallow. One year there was a famine and Mick was faced with starvation. Molly, his wife, urged him to sell their cow at the market in Cork, even though it meant their children would have no milk.

On the long way to Cork Mick met a stranger, a strange fellow with white hair and a wrinkled face, and with a sharp red nose. Mick felt ill at ease. The stranger greeted him

was enraged. "Are you out of your mind?" she shouted.

"Listen to me, Molly, and then you'll realise I've made a good bargain."

His wife listened, impatiently, and at last put a clean cloth on the table and the bottle on the floor.

"Bottle, do your duty," commanded Mick. Immediately two tiny men sprang from the bottle and covered the table with

and, after finding out his plans, offered to buy the cow. "I'll give you this bottle, in exchange."

Mick laughed, in spite of his unease. The stranger looked angry. "This bottle is worth all the cows in Ireland," he shouted, "and besides, your cow may die before you get to Cork." Mick was persuaded that here was a a bargain.

"I agree," he said, "I hope Molly won't be angry with me."

"Angry," said the stranger. "Just tell her to put a clean cloth on the table and put the bottle on the floor. When she tells the bottle to do its duty she'll be surprised at the result."

When Mick showed Molly the bottle (instead of money for the sale of the cow), she

silver and golden dishes, containing the most delicious food. They jumped back into the bottle again. The Mulligan family had a wonderful meal.

The next morning Mick sold some of the dishes in Cork for a lot of money. He bought a cow, a horse and a cart, and beautiful clothes for his wife and children. Every evening the bottle was placed on the floor and told to do its duty.

One day a friend persuaded Mick to lend him the bottle in return for a gift of his farm. Mick soon regretted his folly, because the friend kept the bottle, and Mick became quite poor again. At last he had to take his cow to market to sell. Who should he meet on the way but . . . ?

A

1. What do you think causes a famine?
2. Why did Mick need to sell his cow?
3. Why did Mick laugh at the stranger's offer?
4. What good reason did Molly have for being enraged?
5. What caused her to change her opinion of Mick?
6. How do you think Bottle Hill got its name?

B **Read the story carefully and then use your own words to complete the following sentences:**

1. A legend is a story which . . .
2. The Mulligans were in danger of starving when . . .
3. Because . . . Mrs Mulligan begged Mick to sell the cow.
4. When Mick told him of his intentions, the stranger . . .
5. The stranger became angry because . . .
6. The stranger said the cow might die before . . .
7. Mick had to tell his wife that . . .
8. Mick's wife lost her temper when . . .
9. Although she was very angry she . . .
10. After Mick gave his command two . . .
11. Things went well for the Mulligan family until . . .
12. Shortly after . . . Mick again met the stranger.

C

1. **Pick out the describing words (adjectives) in the first sentence of the second paragraph.**

2. **Here are some nouns and some adjectives. Put the most suitable adjective with each noun:**

Nouns	food	man	clothes	morning	diamonds	corn
Adjectives	golden	impatient	delicious	glittering	gaudy	misty

3. **Write out this passage correctly:**
   mick began to tremble when he saw the odd-looking man again he was afraid to tell him that he had parted with the magic bottle good morning said the man where are you going now poor mick did not know what to say

4. I'm **is a short way of saying** I am.
   Write these in the short way:

I have	you have	we will	he is	we are	they will not

5. **Find out what these words mean:**

legend	exchange	persuade	bargain	result
impatience	realise	contain	regret	delicious

   Use each of the words in a sentence.

D **How do you think the story finished?**

THE FIRST GORILLA HUNT

In the year 1885 an explorer returned from the wilds of Africa. He brought back stories of animals like men and of tribes of dwarfs. No one believed him. This is his own account of the first gorilla hunt.

"We were in hilly, tree-covered country when we saw several gorilla tracks. Our party divided in two so that we could surround the animal when we tracked it to its lair. The trees in the jungle were so closely packed that we often had to creep. Hour after hour we travelled on, on the look-out for our quarry. We heard the chattering of monkeys high in the trees, swinging from branch to branch, and the cries of brightly coloured birds. There were no signs of the gorilla.

Suddenly our native guide clucked his tongue to warn us to be on the alert. The sound of breaking branches could be heard faintly. We all examined our guns. The noise of breaking branches became louder, then suddenly we could see some branches moving. The huge creature was pulling down small trees to reach for their berries and fruits.

For a while there was silence. It was broken by a fearsome sound that filled the forest, scattering birds and small animals in all directions. Into a small clearing we could see ahead there burst a tremendous hairy figure. He stood six feet high, the height of a tall man, with a huge chest and powerful, outstretched arms - a terrifying sight. He pounded his massive breast with his huge hands, the sound resounding like jungle drumbeats. His terrifying roar began like the barking of a savage dog and passed into a deep rumbling like that of distant thunder. As he swayed and roared, his sharp teeth flashed. Slowly he advanced on us until he was six yards away. Just as he appeared about to spring, I levelled my rifle and fired. The immense body dropped in front of me."

A

1. Why did people refuse to believe the explorer?
2. Where did the explorers first see signs of the gorilla?
3. Why do you think the explorer decided to kill a gorilla?
4. What would make it difficult for him to catch the gorilla alive?
5. What plan did the hunters have in mind when they separated?
6. Why were the monkeys high up in the trees?
7. What signs of the gorilla could the hunters see or hear?
8. When did the hunters examine their guns?
9. What frightened the birds and beasts of the jungle?
10. What made the gorilla look so terrifying?

B

1. **Which words in the passage mean the same as the following?**

came back	report	separated	encircle
inspected	upright	extended	beat
echoing	the home of a wild animal		came forward

2. **Choose any six of the above words and then use them in sentences of your own.**

3. **Complete these sentences using these words:**

track	quarry	alert	pound	tribe
divide	appeared	figure	several	lair

   (a) He is going to . . . the money equally among the boys.
   (b) The Sioux are an Indian . . .
   (c) Tom . . . in time for dinner.
   (d) . . . people survived the shipwreck.
   (e) The lion's . . . was full of bones.
   (f) Hunters have to keep . . .
   (g) Hunters keep on after their . . .
   (h) An angry animal might . . . its chest.
   (i) A hunted animal leaves a . . .

4. **The word** account **in the story means a** description **or a** report. **Here are other ways in which the word is used. Pair each phrase with its correct meaning:**

(a) to settle an account	to make good use of
(b) to turn to good account	to pay a bill or charge
(c) to take into account	according to all reports
(d) to account for	of little importance
(e) of little account	because of
(f) on account of	not to pay immediately
(g) to give an account of oneself	to explain
(h) to buy on account	to explain one's actions
(i) by all accounts	to make allowances for

THE FIVE-COLOURED DEER (A Japanese Folk Tale)

Long, long ago, a very rare deer lived in the forest, up in the mountains. No other deer had its white horns and five-coloured coat. No one knew of its existence until a weary traveller fell exhausted into a nearby river. He cried out for help. Only the deer heard him and took pity on him. The noble animal stretched out its horns which the man grasped, and he was pulled to safety.

In gratitude the man exclaimed, "How can I ever repay you? I shall be for ever in your debt."

The deer looked thoughtful and eventually replied, "My coat is very valuable because it is so rare. I have to conceal myself in the forest, away from greedy hunters. You must promise never to reveal my secret hiding place."

"I will not breathe a word to a living soul," the man replied. "Goodbye and thank you."

Sometime later the Queen of that land had a dream. She saw in her dream a marvellous beast - a five-coloured deer with white horns. Nothing would satisfy her, thereafter, but to possess such a magnificent animal. The King offered a huge reward of gold, diamonds, emeralds and rubies to the person who would grant the Queen's request.

The man who had been saved by the deer promised to lead the King's huntsmen to the whereabouts of such an animal. The King was delighted and the hunt was on.

Soon the ungrateful man led the huntsmen to a cave where the unsuspecting beast lay sleeping. The noise of the huntsmen, however, had alarmed a crow, which flew to the deer and bit its ear to warn it of impending danger. The deer, however, was surrounded and there was no escape.

"Who told you of my secret?" the deer asked the King.

"This noble man here," replied the King. "He has earned a handsome reward."

"Noble, indeed, Sir," replied the deer. "I saved that man from drowning and now he has betrayed me. A fine way to repay a debt!"

"A fine way, indeed, noble animal," said the King. "Now you shall go free and he will pay the price of his betrayal, for he is more of an animal than you are."

From that time on no deer were hunted or killed in that land.

A

1. In what way did the deer show his friendship to a stranger?
2. How did the traveller say he would repay his debt?
3. How did he actually "repay his debt"?
4. What do you call a person who betrays a friend?
5. The legend of Fin McCoul on page 52 is full of 'exaggerations'. If the deer had been a person, would this folk story be 'exaggerated'?
6. What sort of 'person' do you think the deer was?
7. What was the deer's secret, and what did the traveller do to betray it?
8. Why did the King of the land want to find the deer?
9. Why did the Queen want to possess the deer?
10. What punishment do you think was given to the traveller for his betrayal?

B

1. **Complete these sentences. You will find the words you need in the story.**
   (a) Things which are not often seen, such as the 'Five-coloured Deer' are very . . .
   (b) A man has skin, an animal has . . .
   (c) If you are tired and do not have rest, you may become quite . . .
   (d) People who are thankful should show . . .
   (e) If a person trusts you, you should not . . . him.
   (f) When we feel sorry for someone, we take . . . on him.
   (g) We can . . . somebody, if we suddenly surprise him.
   (h) If you recover a lost article for someone, you are often entitled to a . . .

2. **Pair the words in the first list with the words in the second list.**
   For example: skin **means** hide; impending **means** coming.

   | skin | tired | extended | clutched | precious |
   | own | reveal | alarmed | impending | enclosed |

   | stretched | valuable | surrounded | coming | exhausted |
   | frightened | disclose | hide | possess | grasped |

3. **Use any six of the above words in sentences of your own.**
4. **Find the words which rhyme with:**

   (a) **white**   and means a sudden fear.
   (b) **rare**   and means a female horse.
   (c) **possess** and means to admit one's guilt.
   (d) **hunt**   and means the sound pigs make.
   (e) **there**   and means free from rain.
   (f) **exist**   and means a cloud of moisture in the air.
   (g) **soul**   and means everything.
   (h) **dream**   and means to appear.
   (i) **price**   and means pleasant.
   (j) **danger** and means a crib.
   (k) **crow**   and means to fling.

VERBS AND ADVERBS

A **Choose suitable** verbs **from the list to fill the empty spaces in the sentences:**

barked	sank	reported	reminded	bandaged	scored
played	became	approached	accepted	determined	invited
witnessed	gave	succeeded	promised		

1. The dog . . . loudly as the postman . . . the house.
2. The nurse . . . his sore leg and . . . him a crutch.
3. Jack . . . in the match and . . . a goal.
4. The sun . . . and it . . . dark.
5. Sue . . . Sandra to her party and she . . .
6. I was . . . to succeed and finally I . . .
7. Jim . . . me that I had . . . to come.
8. Sally . . . the accident that she had . . .

B **Do the same with these adverbs:**

loudly	brightly	gladly	wearily	clearly	speedily
safely	narrowly	slowly	seriously	heavily	easily
suddenly	steadily	carefully	stealthily		

1. The wind howled . . . and the rain fell . . .
2. The sun shone . . . and . . . we welcomed its warming rays.
3. He yawned . . . and . . . rose from his bed.
4. The teacher wrote . . . and we all could . . . read it.
5. Tom ran . . . but was . . . beaten by Donald.
6. The men worked . . . and . . . all day.
7. The burglar crept in . . . , but . . . the lights went on.
8. The soldier was . . . wounded, but he managed to reach his comrades . . .

C **Write down each verb and beside it write the adverb that goes best with it.**

walk	bitterly	cheer	hungrily
speak	attentively	drive	loudly
sing	rapidly	eat	softly
listen	drunkenly	spend	gracefully
play	distinctly	wave	soundly
stagger	seriously	sleep	dangerously
injure	happily	whisper	extravagantly
weep	sweetly	dance	frantically

Choose four verbs from the first list and four from the second list and write sentences using them with suitable adverbs.

WORDS OFTEN CONFUSED

**Here are some words that sound alike but which have different meanings.
Below the list of words there are some sentences. Each sentence has a word
missing. Choose the right word from the list.**

A

one	heard	peace	pain	no	praise
won	herd	piece	pane	know	prays

1. . . . day a strange man came to our house.
2. Our team . . . the football match.
3. In the afternoon we . . . a loud noise.
4. The farmer has a large . . . of cows.
5. The boy ate a large . . . of cake.
6. We all want . . . , not war.
7. John broke a . . . of glass with a stone.
8. I had a . . . in my leg.
9. Dad said he had . . . money.
10. Dad said he did not . . . the stranger.
11. My sister got great . . . for winning the medal.
12. My mother . . . to God every day.

B

tail	seen	hour	missed	some	steel
tale	scene	our	mist	sum	steal

1. The old sailor told me a strange . . .
2. Our dog has a curly . . .
3. I have not . . . Sheila for a week.
4. We stopped to admire the beautiful . . .
5. We have lost . . . dog.
6. We waited an . . . for Colin.
7. We could hardly see through the thick . . .
8. Linda was late and . . . the train.
9. . . . of the questions were very hard.
10. David had only one . . . right.
11. Good people never . . .
12. These knives are made of stainless . . .

C   Write sentences of your own using these words:

here	meat	pair	write	hole	past
hear	meet	pear	right	whole	passed

D   Rewrite these sentences, choosing the right word from the brackets.
1. I am going to (wait, weight) for John.
2. Mr Baker's house is for (sail, sale).
3. We have (too, two) dogs in our house.
4. I am going to have a (stake, steak) for my dinner.

ALL SORTS

A Join these sentences with and or but:
1. I rang the door bell. I was admitted at once.
2. I went to the concert. I did not like it.
3. Mother bought a new dress. She never wore it.
4. I went to the football match. I found it very exciting.
5. I went to the football match. It was not a good game.
6. Dad wrote a letter. He posted it this morning.

B Rewrite the following sentences, putting in the correct word:

who	whose	whom	which

1. The police questioned the man . . . shop had been burgled.
2. The dog . . . won the prize was sold.
3. This is the gentleman from . . . I received the money.
4. I do not know the boy . . . was at the door.
5. I saw the man . . . house had been on fire.
6. To . . . did you give the parcel?
7. . . . is going with you to the cinema?
8. Did you see the bull . . . the farmer bought?

C Here is a list of containers and below it a list of the things you might find in them. Now write sentences telling what you would expect to find in each container.
Examples: A bottle may hold milk.
A wardrobe is used for holding clothes.

tank	bin	cask	wardrobe	wallet	caddy
bottle	till	vase	brief-case	cruet	bucket

money	rubbish	pound notes	flowers	tea	papers
petrol	clothes	salt and pepper	wine	milk	water

D Rewrite the following, putting in capital letters, full stops, inverted commas, and so on:
1. where are you going linda asked her mother
2. did you lose many sheep in the storm jim asked the farmer
3. no I was lucky replied the farmer I lost only two
4. stand where you are shouted the policeman
5. as she opened the door doris exclaimed what a lovely day

E Write these sentences, putting in the apostrophe:
1. Janes dress is in her aunts house.
2. I cant play football because Ive a sore foot.
3. The girl couldnt write as shed no pencil.
4. Dads car is in my friends garage.
5. youre sure to meet him if he isn't late.

THE STORY OF THE FISHERMAN (1)

There was once an old fisherman who was very poor. Early every morning he went out to his usual employment, but he made it a rule of his life never to cast his net into the sea more than four times a day.

One morning before sunrise he cast his net three times. The first time, all that was in the net was the dead body of an ass; the second time, he drew only a basket of sand and mud, and on the third occasion he brought out some heavy stones and shells. He was very disappointed, and shook his head sadly.

It was now dawn, and, as was his custom, he said his prayers. Then he cast his net for the fourth time. Again there were no fish, but caught in the net was a heavy vase of yellow copper, shut up and fastened with lead. He examined the vase, and shook it, but he could hear nothing. Yet he was certain that it contained something.

He cut round the lead with his knife and opened it. Then he turned it upside down - but nothing came out.

He set it down on the ground, and, while he was gazing at it, thick smoke came from the vase.

The smoke gradually rose almost to the clouds and spread over the water and shore like a thick cloud. Then it slowly came together again and took the form of a gigantic genie . . .

1. What was the rule of the fisherman's life?
2. How many times did he cast his net before sunrise?
3. What did he catch on each occasion?
4. Why was he very disappointed?
5. The old fisherman was very poor. Name two things he might have done with the fish if he had caught any.
6. Why was he so sure that the vase contained something important?
7. What was the fisherman accustomed to doing at dawn?
8. Describe the vase that the fisherman caught.

M.E.4–D

THE STORY OF THE FISHERMAN (2)

. . . As you may imagine, the fisherman would have liked to run away, but he was rooted to the spot with fear.

"Humble yourself before me," exclaimed the genie, "or I will kill you."

"Why?" answered the fisherman. "Have I not set you free? Will you return evil for good?"

"I cannot allow you to live," said the genie, "as you will understand when you hear my story. King Solomon shut me up in this bottle for refusing to obey him and had the bottle cast into the sea. During the first century of my imprisonment, I vowed that I would make anyone who set me free very rich. Alas, no one drew me out. At length I became so enraged that I vowed that I would without mercy kill whoever released me. I cannot break my vow."

"Since I cannot escape death," said the poor fisherman, "I must ask you something first. Were you really in that vase? I can hardly believe it."

"I swear it," said the genie.

"Then prove it," cried the fisherman.

The genie instantly turned into smoke and slowly disappeared back into the vase. Quickly, the old man put the lead cover back on and the genie was again imprisoned.

The genie pleaded with the fisherman to let him out, but the fisherman refused until the genie promised not to harm him and to reward him handsomely.

So the fisherman took off the lead cover and out came the genie. The genie then took him to a lake far away over high mountains.

"Throw in your net," ordered the genie.

The fisherman did so and drew out four fishes - one red, one blue, one yellow, one white.

"Take them to the Sultan's palace," said the genie, "and he will give you more money than you have ever had in your life."

The old fisherman did so and the Sultan gave him four hundred pieces of gold. Even more, the Sultan promised to pay the same every day for other fish of the same kind. So the poor fisherman became very rich.

A

1. Why do you think the fisherman was terrified?
2. Which phrase in the story tells you that he was afraid?
3. Was the genie being fair or unfair in deciding to kill the fisherman? What did the fisherman think? Which sentence in the story tells you?
4. What trick did the fisherman play on the genie?
5. How do you think the genie felt when he was tricked?
6. Do you think the fisherman was a very clever person? Give a reason for your answer.
7. How did the fisherman become rich?
8. What is a Sultan? Give other names of other kinds of rulers.

B

1. Appeared **and** disappeared **are opposites.**
Use the prefixes dis un in im **to give the opposites of:**

> able possible seen cover polite correct honest proper direct
> distinct equal grateful mobile disposed well hospitable

IT'S DYNAMITE

An explosives alert closed the Forth Road Bridge recently. Two teenagers had discovered gelignite on a rock face overhanging the bridge.

While police and Army bomb disposal experts raced to the scene, Andrew, one of the boys, told how he walked home about a mile with a stick of gelignite in his hand. He had been climbing on the rocks near the bridge, and a piece of paper caught his eye. It was sticking out of a hole on a ledge 50 feet above the M90. "We pulled it out and found what looked like a spent cartridge," he said to the newspaper reporter. "Then I noticed another piece of paper in the same hole and pulled that out. Out came what looked like a wet sausage. I had a fair idea that it could be dynamite, but I never really thought it was dangerous."

On his arrival home, Andrew showed his find to his father, who immediately advised him to contact the police. Army bomb disposal men were alerted. They found the gelignite, on examination, to be in a "highly dangerous state". It was later detonated. The bomb disposal squad made an immediate search of the area where the boys found it. . . . The police sealed off a section of the Forth Bridge approach roads so that the bomb team could make a more detailed search of the borehole. . . .

A spokesman for the police announced, "More gelignite has been discovered and we have taken the precaution of stopping traffic."

The fear was well-founded because in the explosion that followed the normally busy motorway was showered with rocks. The police were satisfied that the gelignite was left years ago by workmen engaged in building the bridge approach roads. A considerable amount of rock-blasting was done in their work.

The police have successfully dealt with the danger and have issued a statement. "This is a warning to anyone not to touch anything in these circumstances. They should inform the police immediately and keep well away."

A
1. What did the "wet sausage" turn out to be?
2. Why is it called a banger?
3. Why was the Forth Road Bridge closed for a time?
4. What did the police do in the emergency?
5. What advice did Andrew's father offer?
6. What are bomb disposal men supposed to do?
7. In what ways can the police help them?
8. What further danger did the police fear?
9. What kinds of explosives are mentioned in the account?

B Make nouns from these words:

explode	close	discover	decide	advise
dangerous	dispose	describe	detonate	think

C Imagine that you have found a bottle of poison and taken it home. Give an account of the emergency which followed. Make an interesting headline.

FIN McCOUL - The Hebridean Hercules

The Scots originally came over from Ireland. Many of their folk tales tell of legendary Irish heroes performing marvellous deeds. These legends have been passed down from father to son over hundreds of years. They contain some truth and a lot of exaggeration due to fertile imaginations. Everybody loves a story, especially one about deeds which become more and more stupendous as they are retold.

One such astonishing story relates the incredible, marvellous adventures of Fin

killed, and running away and being disgraced. He consulted his fairy wife, Oonagh.

She devised a cunning plan to outwit Cuchullain. She knew that his strength lay in the middle finger of his right hand. Oonagh baked a loaf of bread and put some stones in it. She dressed Fin as her infant son and put him in a cradle.

Cuchullain came along shouting and uttering threats and challenges, furious at not meeting his rival. Oonagh offered him

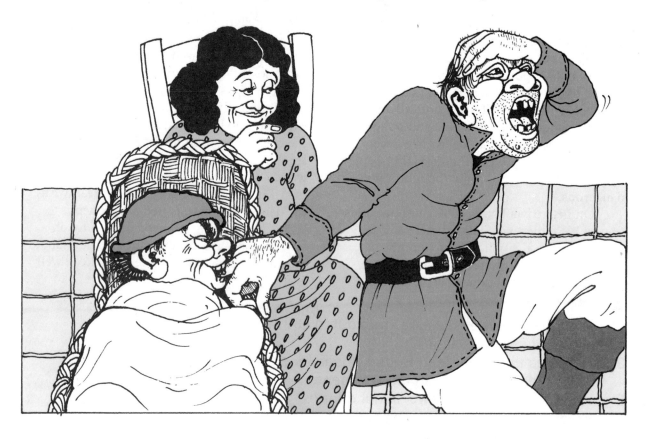

McCoul, King of Tara and a renowned war-leader. Fin was reputed to be a giant of a man who made a bridge from Ireland to Scotland which is still known as the "Giant's Causeway".

Another gigantic hero of the time was Cuchullain. Fin was alarmed when he heard that the dreaded Cuchullain was seeking a match of strength. He was in a dilemma, that is he had to choose between staying and being

hospitality. He bit her loaf and broke his teeth. Oonagh secretly changed the stony loaf for a soft one and gave it to Fin the "infant", who quickly bolted it down. Cuchullain was amazed and worried. He reached out his right hand to feel the teeth of this terrible infant. At that moment Fin bit off his middle finger and Cuchullain collapsed and died.

"Mother" and "infant" celebrated their success far into the night.

A

1. The Hebrides are islands off the coast of Scotland. Hercules was a legendary giant. Why was Fin McCoul called the "Hebridean Hercules"?
2. A legend is a story of long ago that has some truth in it. Do you think Fin McCoul was a King of Tara?
3. Why do we not really believe he built the "Giant's Causeway"?
4. What was the terrible choice Fin McCoul had to make?
5. What do you think he actually said to his wife?
6. What do you think Oonagh said to him?
7. What makes you think Oonagh was superstitious?
8. What plan did she think up?
9. Why could Fin McCoul see Cuchullain but Cuchullain could not see him?
10. Why was Cuchullain impressed by the "baby boy"?

B

1. **Match the words and phrases in the first group with those in the second group:**

> brave people   in the beginning   wonderful
> hundreds of years   making something appear bigger
> fruitful   famous   match of strength

> originally   centuries   contest   exaggerate
> fertile   heroes   marvellous   renowned

2. **Which word or words mean the same as:**

(a) wonderful	marvellous	stupendous	amazing	lovely
(b) origin	early	beginning	start	once
(c) perform	act	do	move	permit
(d) incredible	creditable	unbelievable	false	wrong
(e) alarmed	aroused	frightened	disturbed	scared
(f) dreaded	feared	afraid	fearsome	deadly
(g) disgraced	graceful	ungrateful	dishonoured	shamed
(h) changed	switched	turned	altered	reversed

3. **Complete these sentences. The words in the story will help you.**
   (a) Old stories of heroes are often . . . because of people's imaginations.
   (b) They . . . the adventures of legendary heroes.
   (c) Fin McCoul had the . . . of being a giant.
   (d) Since Fin could not make up his own mind he . . . to consult his wife.
   (e) Oonagh outwitted Cuchullain by . . . a trick on him.
   (f) Cuchullain . . . Fin with violence and . . . him to fight.
   (g) People show hospitality to strangers and travellers by offering them . . .
   (h) When a person has done well, he likes to . . . his success.
   (i) By changing his appearance a person can . . . himself.
   (j) A person who competes against another is called a . . .

MODOC COMES TO TOWN

Fabian Redwood, once a circus trainer, and now a retired old gentleman of 76, stared at a heading in the Kansas Times: MODOC COMES TO TOWN. Memories of half a century ago flooded into Fabian's mind. There he was, young, handsome, fearless, the star of Ringling Brothers' Circus, patting affectionately the trunk of his co-star, Modoc. He could see names in lights of the show's greatest attraction, the wonderful double act, "Redwood and Modoc".

Fabian limped down to the showground on the outskirts of Kansas and asked an official if he could see Modoc. The surprised official refused. "Strangers upset the animals," he said curtly, "and Modoc is very temperamental."

"Me a stranger!" gasped Fabian. "Rubbish! Modoc and I worked together for years. She'll never forget me."

Fabian persuaded the official to take him to Modoc. The results of the meeting were unbelievable. Old, lean and bent as he was, the moment he appeared the 77 year old creature squealed in delight. There was a joyful reunion. Fabian thought of bygone years and he smartly commanded, "Trunk up, Modoc." In an instant the great beast reared on her hind legs and flung her trunk up high. Then to the astonishment of the onlookers Modoc gently put her trunk round the old man and hoisted him level with her eyes so that she could gaze into his face.

The circus folk cheered and clapped this show of affection, and Fabian burst into tears. Later he said, "An animal does what a trainer wants out of respect or love. Modoc and I recognised each other instantly even though I no longer look the way I did, nor does she."

Modoc, because of her splendid body and intelligence, appeared over the years in Hollywood films, such as 'Daktari'. Her most heroic moment, however, came some thirty years ago when a disastrous fire destroyed the Ringling Brothers' Big Top, killing a hundred and sixty people.

During the blaze Modoc returned again and again to help the circus hands drag cageloads of frightened animals to safety.

When Fabian and Modoc had their amazing reunion the first thing he noticed was the scarred trunk and ears. The dark brown blotches had not been there when they were parted in 1922.

A

1. This story appeared in a Sunday newspaper. What makes you think it could be true?
2. In what ways do you think the young Fabian is now different from the old Fabian?
3. In what ways do you think Modoc has changed over the years?
4. What do you think has not changed over the years in Fabian and Modoc?
5. Could Modoc have appeared successfully in a single act?
6. How did Fabian help Modoc to become famous?
7. How did Modoc help Fabian to become famous?
8. Why do you think Modoc put her trunk round Fabian?
9. Why did the acrobats and jugglers and dancers clap their hands?
10. What kind of animals are chosen for films such as 'Daktari'?
11. What happened to the Ringling Brothers' Big Top?
12. How did Modoc help during the fire?

B Complete these sentences:

1. (a) A person who has stopped working because of age is . . .
   (b) The star of a show is the main . . .
   (c) People who show love are said to be . . .
   (d) The parts of a town away from the centre are suburbs or . . .
   (e) A person in charge is called an . . .

2. **Write down the opposites of:**

fearless	handsome	calm	remember	stupid	young
straight	joyful	love	depart	double	safety

3. **Match the words in the first panel with the words in the second panel which mean the same:**

affection	persuade	fearless	gaze	amazing
annoy	laboured	order	marked	observe

stare	torment	command	scarred	worked
love	astonishing	brave	notice	coax

4. **Make nouns from the following:**

persuade	retire	raise	respectful	heroic	true
recognise	unite	intelligent	disastrous	appear	famous

5. **Make adjectives from the following:**

memory	surprise	delight	astonishment	love	fright
affection	belief	joy	gently	blaze	scar

6. **Imagine you are a reporter at the circus fire. Make a startling headline and tell the story of Modoc's heroism.**

GULLIVER IN LILLIPUT

This story is taken from a famous book called 'Gulliver's Travels'. Dr Gulliver was a ship's doctor who went on a long voyage and was the only survivor after the ship was wrecked. Gulliver was washed ashore on an island and fell asleep exhausted. Here, he tells us what happened the following day.

"I attempted to rise but was not able to stir. I found my arms and legs were strongly fastened and my hair tied down in the same way. I felt several slender threads across my body from my armpits to my thighs. I could only look upwards. The sun began to grow hot and the light hurt my eyes.

In a little time I felt something alive moving on my left leg. It advanced gently forward over my breast and came almost up to my chin. Bending my eyes downward as much as I could, I saw a human creature not six inches high, with a bow and arrow in his hands and a quiver on his back. In the meantime I felt at least forty more of the same kind following on the first. I was so astonished and roared so loudly that they all ran back in fright.

At length, struggling to get loose, I had the good fortune to break the strings and wrench out the pegs that fastened my left hand to the ground. With a violent pull, which gave me great pain, I managed to loosen the strings that tied down my hair on the left side, so that I was able to turn my head about two inches.

There was a great shout and I felt about a hundred arrows discharged on my left hand which pricked me like so many needles. I thought it was wise to lie still. When the people observed that I was quiet they shot no more arrows."

Later, however, Gulliver came to be liked and trusted by the King and the people of Lilliput. They called him the Man Mountain. When their enemies from the island of Blefescu were ready to invade Lilliput, Gulliver saved the day for the Lilliputians.

He waded into the sea and hastened towards Blefescu. The enemy shook with fright at the sight of the huge figure striding through the sea. They tried bravely to save their ships, showering Gulliver with thousands of tiny arrows. He put on his spectacles to protect his eyes. Next he fixed hooks on strings to all the fifty ships of the enemy fleet and dragged them back to Lilliput.

On his return the coast of Lilliput was lined with tiny figures, waving and cheering. Gulliver was given a tremendous welcome as a national hero.

A

1. Is this a true story?
2. Why do you think it is fiction?
3. How did Gulliver become a castaway?
4. Tell about the survivors from the shipwreck.
5. Tell why Gulliver was unable to rise.
6. What effect did the sunlight have on Gulliver?
   Complete these sentences:
7. Gulliver roared loudly because . . .
8. As a result of his roaring the little men . . .
9. When the arrows struck him Gulliver decided . . .
10. After . . . the tiny men shot no more arrows.
11. The people of Lilliput . . . because of his huge size.
12. On seeing Gulliver the enemy . . .
13. Gulliver saved the day by . . .
14. Because of Gulliver's brave deeds the people of Lilliput . . .

B
1. **What words in the story mean the following?**

very tired	tried	thin	went forward	surprised
pull out	was able	noticed	attack	hurried

2. **Write this passage correctly, putting in capital letters and full stops:**
   gulliver spoke to one of his captors he indicated with his hand that he was hungry he was given baskets of meat and barrels of wine a message from the king soon arrived

3. **Write sentences about each of the following to tell who they are and what they do:**

author	captive	captor	archer	giant	dwarf
invader	hero	castaway	inhabitant	citizen	enemy

C Gulliver had more adventures when he arrived in Brobdingnag, the land of the giants. Imagine you are Gulliver and tell of your first meeting with the giants.

D Imagine you are one of the giants and tell how you felt when you first saw Gulliver.

E Where would you rather go - to Lilliput or to Brobdingnag? Why?

BIRD WATCHING

Sandra and Kay have an interesting hobby. They are bird watchers. In their spare time they cycle across the sea-lying parts of Norfolk. There are wide areas of marshy ground and some hills. They like to leave their bicycles near the top of one hill and make their way very carefully on to a high ledge. The wind is usually bitterly cold, but they wear thick pullovers and anoraks.

On a clear day the view is magnificent. Above, on the craggy ledges on the high hills, they can see almost every feather on the peewits and below, in the salt marshes near the river where it enters the sea, they have a close-up view of the gannets, moorhens, sandpipers, snipe, heron, kingfishers and plovers.

The birds fly, feed, nest, preen their feathers, strut about and guard their young. No human being disturbs the wildlife in this area. Unlike cage-birds the different species of birds dive, swoop, hover, glide and soar in a most natural way. Each species has its own habits and likings. Nature has equipped them for their particular purposes. The heron has long legs for standing in water and a long sharp beak for catching fish. The eagle falcon has a strong curved beak and a huge wing span. It swoops down on unsuspecting mice, rabbits and even lambs. Like other birds of prey it has hooked talons for gripping its victims.

Sandra and Kay are able to observe all these natural activities at close range. They have bought powerful binoculars from their savings. Sandra is very skilful at taking photographs of birds in their natural state. Kay prefers to sketch them on her pad and paint the pictures later in water colour.

A

1. A . . . is something you do in your spare time out of interest.
2. People who observe birds are known as . . .
3. Sandra and Kay wear warm clothing because . . .
4. They have a close-up view of the birds although . . .
5. Sandra obtains pictures of the birds by . . . while Kay . . .

B

1. **Which words in the passage mean the same as the following?**

watch	free	cautiously	goes into	sight	defend
upsets	type	rise up	customs	fitted	special
seizing	actions	purchased	would rather	field-glasses	

2. **What are the opposites of the following?**

interesting	usual	artificial	same	general
natural	blunt	straight	powerful	skilful	spend

C **Some words mean very nearly the same as each other. Two of the three words in the brackets are synonyms. Can you find them in each sentence?**

1. Tell the truth and do not (reject, deceive, mislead) me.
2. Do not (abandon, depart, leave) me when I need your help.
3. I want you to (aid, assist, resist) me with my school work.
4. The storm (raged, spoiled, damaged) the flowers in the garden.
5. I cannot (last, progress, advance) further without a rest.
6. The referee will (separate, prepare, part) the two boxers.
7. Rip Van Winkle was too old to (alter, change, improve) his ways.
8. Robert's parents (commanded, ordered, allowed) him to stay at home.
9. Mary's parents (expected, let, permitted) her to go to the party.
10. Has the dentist (extracted, examined, inspected) your teeth?
11. A microscope is useful for (repairing, enlarging, magnifying) small objects.
12. The detective (revealed, concluded, showed) how the theft had taken place.
13. Many people (collect, sell, gather) stamps as a hobby.
14. Shops (sell, show, display) many kinds of goods in their windows.

D **Group Terms**

gang	army	team	crew	choir	class	staff	shoal	deck
pack	herd	horde	troop	nest	gaggle	litter	flock	

Choose from the list the correct words to complete the following:

a . . . of thieves	a . . . of sailors	an . . . of soldiers
a . . . of singers	a . . . of wasps	a . . . of geese
a . . . of bees	a . . . of pups	a . . . of cattle
a . . . of footballers	a . . . of pupils	a . . . of sheep
a . . . of monkeys	a . . . of teachers	a . . . of wolves
a . . . of herring	a . . . of savages	a . . . of cards

SENTENCE MAKING - Using Present Participles

A **Another way to join sentences is to change the verb in the first sentence into a word ending with** ing.
Look at these sentences: I crept up behind him.

I touched him on the shoulder.
They can be joined, like this:

Creeping up behind him, I touched him on the shoulder.
Combine the following sentences in this way:
1. I heard a loud cry. I turned round quickly.
2. She burst into tears. She rushed out of the room.
3. He threw off his coat. He jumped into the water.
4. I looked out of the window. I saw a man at the gate.
5. She opened the door. She called to the boy to come back.
6. I entered the house. I saw my mother lying on the floor.
7. I heard a noise. I rushed out.
8. I placed my prize on the table. I smiled broadly.

B **Now look at these two sentences:** The dog barked furiously.

It bounded after the burglar.
When joined they make this sentence:

Barking furiously, the dog bounded after the burglar.
In this case we have dropped It **in the second sentence and put** the dog **in its place.**
Now join these sentences in the same way:
1. The lady **picked** up her umbrella. She went out into the rain.
2. The girl **wept** bitterly. She told me she had lost her purse.
3. The boy **lifted** a stone. He threw it at the cat.
4. The sailor **led** me to the harbour. He showed me his ship.
5. The tramp placed his bundle on the seat. He lay down on the grass.
6. The accused man confessed everything. He pleaded for mercy.
7. The motorist travelled at great speed. He arrived in good time.
8. The girl saw smoke coming through the window. She gave the alarm.

C **Sometimes we change the verb in the second sentence into an** ing **word.**
Look at these sentences: My mother went out.

She took her purse with her.
They may be joined to make this sentence:

My mother went out, taking her purse with her.
Now join these sentences in this way:
1. We saw a man. He fished in the river.
2. I walked home. I felt very tired.
3. The girl walked along. She sang happily.
4. We saw a large snake. It wriggled through the grass.
5. The boys watched the fishermen. They mended their nets.

SENTENCE MAKING

Look at these three sentences:

> The farmer was in the field.
> A fox entered the farmyard.
> It carried off a duck.

These sentences may be combined to make one sentence, like this:

While the farmer was in the field, a fox entered the farmyard and carried off a duck.

Now combine the following sentences in any way you please. Do not use and **more than once in any sentence:**

A 1. I was watching TV. A small boy opened the door. He ran into the room crying bitterly. (Begin with 'As')
  2. I was walking to the bus stop. I met a man. He was carrying a heavy bag. (Begin with 'As')
  3. The rain stopped. The boys ran out. They found the road flooded. (Begin with 'When')
  4. Everyone loved the boy. He was always courteous. He was afraid of nothing.
  5. The children ran to the woods. They found the dog. It was lying under a tree.

B 1. The boy lifted a stone. He threw it at the dog. It was barking at him.
  2. The boy had recovered from a severe illness. He was sent to a farm. He stayed there for four weeks. (Begin with 'After')
  3. We stood on the bridge. We saw a boat. It was sailing up the river.
  4. The stranger arrived at the station. He hired a taxi. He asked to be taken to the nearest hotel.
  5. The boy was walking to the seashore. He passed a fisherman. He was carrying a large salmon.

C 1. The train left. The man lifted his luggage. He hurried from the station.
  2. Ethel was sweeping the floor. She found the ring. Her mother had lost it.
  3. I met the lady. I shook hands with her. I asked her when she had arrived in this country.
  4. The guard blew his whistle. We waved to our friends. They had come to see us off.
  5. The men were crossing the loch. A storm blew up. Their boat was nearly capsized. (Begin with 'While')

D 1. The prisoner came into court. He confessed. He had stolen the bag.
  2. I entered the building. I saw a man. He appeared to be acting in a very strange manner.
  3. The thief robbed a jeweller's shop. He was caught by a policeman. He was boarding a bus.
  4. We walked along the river bank. We watched two boys. They were fishing.
  5. The doctor examined the man. He had been knocked down by a bus. He found that his leg was broken.

ALL SORTS

A   **Join these sentences by** who, whom, whose **or** which:
1. The little girl was crying. Her doll was broken.
2. The man was arrested by the police. He had broken into the bank.
3. The gentleman has arrived. We were expecting him.
4. I put away the book. I had been reading it.
5. I visited the lady. Her house had been burgled.
6. Mr Jones is a Welshman. Everybody likes him.

B   **Punctuate the following:**
1. what have you done demanded my father
2. it was an accident I replied
3. I am not going to school said Helen because I am not well
4. did you see my father's new car asked Mary
5. help help exclaimed Jack I can't move
6. our car is bigger than yours boasted Hilary

C   **Put the words in brackets in their proper places:**
1. (peace, piece) Mother will get no . . . until Bob gets a . . . of cake.
2. (their, there) . . . were many people in . . . houses.
3. (too, two) The . . . girls were . . . tired to walk.
4. (allowed, aloud) We were not . . . to talk . . .
5. (flour, flower) Mother brought home a beautiful . . . and a bag of . . .
6. (hole, whole) The . . . load of sand was put into a deep . . .

D   **Rewrite these sentences in the plural and change the verbs to the past tense:**
1. The knife has a sharp blade.
2. The child feels the cold very much.
3. The woman dearly loves children.
4. The man wears a light overcoat.
5. I intend to buy a new car.
6. The fox is put in a box.
7. The mouse bites the cheese.
8. The teacher scolds the boy.
9. The girl is sick.
10. The cat plays with the ball.
11. You buy a lollipop.
12. I am going swimming.

E   **If you put these groups of words in their correct order they will make good sentences. Start each sentence with a capital letter.**
1. the postman   as I went along the street   I met
2. if I could show him the way to the station   asked me   the stranger
3. coming up the river   as we stood on the bridge   we saw a boat
4. returned to their homes   the people sheltering   when the storm ceased   under a tree
5. into court   he confessed   when the prisoner came   that he had committed the crime
6. he noticed   was on fire   as he approached the house that the chimney

ALL SORTS

A **Only one of the words in the bracket is correct. Write each sentence using the correct word.**
1. Lorna and Linda (is, are) very clever.
2. Alfred (are, is) going to London.
3. One of my friends (are, is) meeting me at the bus stop.
4. Two policemen (was, were) looking for the man.
5. Bert and Jack (has, have) won prizes.
6. One of the boys (has, have) arrived.

B **Write these sentences, putting in inverted commas:**
1. The sea was very calm said Robert.
2. The boys took a great risk said my mother.
3. I think it was a simple accident replied Dennis.
4. Perhaps it was replied my father.

C **Choose the best verbs from the list to complete the sentences:**

| crossed | arrived | thumped | strolled | shocked |

1. Dad . . . the table with his fist.
2. Jim . . . at the station in good time.
3. We . . . the railway by the bridge.
4. I was . . . to hear of the accident.
5. The man . . . across the playing field.

D **Complete each comparison by using the correct word from the list:**

| honey | lion | peacock | feather | coal | fiddle |

as black as . . .   as brave as a . . .   as sweet as . . .
as proud as a . . .   as light as a . . .   as fit as a . . .

E **Write the following correctly:**
doctor william blake   sir robert lang
captain james robertson   long road brighton
preston street manchester   dover avenue margate

F **Put these words in the correct places in the story:**

| returned | supported | finest | declared | match | scored |

When my brother . . . from the football . . . he . . . that it was the . . . game he had seen for a long time. The team he . . . had . . . four goals.

G **Join the correct parts to make sensible sentences:**
1. The girls hurried home   unless you can give a good excuse.
2. The postman handed me a letter   wherever I go.
3. You will be punished   as I was leaving the house.
4. Buster, my dog, follows me   because it was late.

ALL SORTS

A **Answer these questions in good sentences. Use your dictionary if you do not know the meaning of any of the words.**
1. Would an aggressive person be timid?
2. Does a thrifty person spend his money foolishly?
3. Is wholesome food good or bad for you?
4. Is a jovial person mournful or happy?
5. A man's salary starts at £2000 a year and goes up to £4250 a year. What is his maximum salary and what is his minimum?
6. What kind of jobs do most people prefer - temporary or permanent ones?

B **Improve the following sentences by changing the order of the words:**
1. The boy was warned by the teacher who was making a noise.
2. The vase cost three pounds which I gave to my aunt.
3. The book was called Robinson Crusoe which I bought.
4. The bus was just leaving the bus station which we hoped to catch.
5. The friend has beautiful furniture with whom I was staying.
6. The lady told me she came from Italy to whom I was speaking.

C **Find one word that means the same as:**

to give a little laugh	to eat quickly
to walk very slowly	to speak softly
to run quickly	to gather together
to go out of sight	to make bright

D **Combine the following sentences to make one good sentence. Do not use** and **more than once in any sentence.**
1. I looked up. I saw an old man. He was carrying a bundle on his back.
2. Everyone loved the boy. He always spoke the truth. He was afraid of nothing.
3. I opened the door. I saw a boy. He was sitting in an armchair.
4. The rain stopped. The boys ran out. They found the field flooded.   (Begin with 'When')
5. The little girl was carried away. She screamed loudly. She kicked her legs furiously.   (Begin with 'As')
6. The children ran to the woods. They found the dog. It was lying asleep under a tree.
7. The boys opened the front door. They called their cat. She was sitting on the wall.
8. We rushed along the platform. The train was pulling out of the station. We just missed it. (Begin with 'Although')

E **There should be three sentences in the following passage. Rewrite it, putting in the capital letters and full stops:**
tom fell into the river he was a good swimmer and struck out strongly for the bank in spite of the strong current the boy was able to reach it without much difficulty

TWO PICTURE STORIES

Here is a two picture story. The pictures show an exciting event. The story begins with a leading sentence. Make other sentences to tell the rest of the story. You can use some of the words given. Try to find a good title for your story.

Fog came down very suddenly in the North Sea.

trawler	fishing trip	fog
engine trouble	adrift	danger
rocks	warning	
lighthouse flashes		

high waves	fierce wind	
pitching	tossing	S.O.S.
flares	lifeboat	bravery
rescue		

Now try making another story from these pictures. The first sentence is given below, and some of the words you can use. Make up a title for your story.

A party of climbers were all set to climb Ben Nevis.

winter	clothing	anoraks
boots	equipment	packs
axes	ropes	binoculars
ascend	steep	route

rocky	ledge	difficult
foothold	slip	drop
suspended	hauled	safety
continue	top	success

TWO PICTURE STORIES

This two picture story is about a highwayman called **Dick Turpin** and his horse **Black Bess**. Tell what happens in your own way. Use the sentences and words given below. Try to think of a title for your story.

The stagecoach set out on the road from Portsmouth to London.

driver	guard	passengers	alarm
pistol shot	warning	demanded	
money	jewels	terrified	obeyed

Soldiers suddenly appeared in the distance.

noise	horses' hooves	shouting
soldiers	charge	leap
wall	escape	chase

Do the same with this two picture story. It is about a mutiny on board the pirate ship **Black Hawk**. This time no words are given to help you. See if you can find your own words with which to tell this story.

GONE CAMPING

This picture tells a story. Begin your story with the sentence given. Then continue the story in your own way. You can use some of the words below.
During the summer holidays Harry and Dick decided to go camping.

packs	equipment	train	country	fields
trees	fences	animals	pitch tent	wood
camp fire	cooking	exploring	tired	sleep

VISIT TO A PET SHOP

Now tell this story in the same way.
It was Robert's birthday.

Father	Emily	surprise	visit	shopkeeper
doorway	choose	pet	attracted	friendly
puppy	price	purchase	pleased	home

SUNK BY AN ICEBERG!

Look at these three pictures. Each picture tells part of a story. The first picture shows the liner Titanic sailing across the Atlantic Ocean. The other two pictures show what happened to the liner. Can you tell the story from these pictures in your own words?

SHIPWRECKED!

Sometimes people are shipwrecked and land on a desert island. Can you imagine that you are stranded on a desert island with one friend who is injured? Look at the pictures and tell what you did when your ship sank.

THE WILD STALLION

Look carefully at these pictures and answer the questions below. Then see if you can make an exciting story out of the pictures.

1. What makes you think that these horses are not tame?
2. What do the horses do when a cowboy comes near?
3. What does the cowboy try to do?
4. Why do cowboys want to capture wild horses?
5. Where does the cowboy take the captured horse?
6. What is a - ranch, ranch-house, corral?
7. What does the horse do when the cowboy tries to break it in?
8. What often happens to the rider?
9. What is a horse like after it has been broken in?

SUSPECTS ARRESTED

Look carefully at these pictures and answer the questions. Then write a story from the pictures.

1. Who are the two men in the picture?
2. What do you think they have done?
3. What are they doing now?
4. What made the policeman suspicious?
5. What did the policeman decide to do?
6. What did the men do when the policeman approached them?
7. How did the men try to escape?
8. Why did another policeman appear on the road?
9. What did this policeman attempt to do?
10. How do you think the story ended?

FOUR PICTURE STORY

These pictures tell a story. It begins with a boy and his sister going to a boating pond. Perhaps you can say why they went there and what happens. Give your story a title.

The words in the panel below may help you with your story.

Easter	sunshine	visit	boating-pond	yacht
wind	middle	excited	attempt	reach
balance	sister	rescue	steer	

Give the children names and try to make your story exciting.

CHILDREN TO THE RESCUE

?

Here is another story told in pictures. In the first picture an old lady is waving for help from a high window. What happens in the other pictures? You will notice that there is no last picture. Can you give an ending to this story either by drawing the last picture or by saying what should be in it?

Now write the complete story. The words below might help you.

treatment	first aid	injury
telephone	doctor	visit
ambulance	hospital	wheel-chair
relations	happy	recovery
thankful	children	street

STORY OUTLINES

Begin with the sentences given and make good stories following the outline given.

1. Hundreds of people turned out to watch the circus procession.

    | Ringmaster | band | performers | costumes | cages |
    | animals | noise | cheering | excitement |

2. The heavy rain forced the campers to rush for shelter.

    | clouds | darkness | downpour | lightning | flooding |
    | wet clothes | farmhouse | shelter | warmth | food |

3. We woke early on Christmas Day.

    | excited | bright | cheerful | expecting | surprises |
    | presents | tree | greetings | dinner | party | visits |

4. My grandparents live in another town.

    | train | visit | pleased | welcome | kind | stories |
    | photographs | cakes and lemonade | farewell |

5. Neddy the donkey works on a sandy beach.

    | summer | master | charges | rides | slow | gentle |
    | patient | children | favourite | sugar lumps | reward |

6. Harry scored the winning goal for his school.

    | match | friendly | players | field | toss | wind |
    | teams | evenly matched | no score | second half | long pass |
    | header | goal | final whistle |

7. A fire broke out in a baker's shop in Duke Street.

    | passer-by | notice | flames | smoke | smell | telephone |
    | Fire Brigade | engines | hoses | damage | no injuries |

8. While reading about the space craft's moon landing, Neill fell asleep.

    | dream | spaceman | rocket | launched | flight | space |
    | landing | craters | creatures | advance | no escape |
    | awakening | relief |

9. Here is what my best friend is like.

    | tall | fair-haired | pale-faced | freckled | neat |
    | well-dressed | good-humoured | talkative | agreeable | loyal |

STORY OUTLINES

1. Ernie and Eva travel to school by bus.

stop	queue	upstairs	crowded	sights	lights
traffic	buildings	sounds	horns	bells	brakes
coughs	"Fares Please"	conductor	tickets		

2. Tim's hobby is collecting foreign stamps.

Album	packets	two hundred	forty pence		
many countries	sorts	hinges	sticks	builds	
collection					

3. Yesterday was full of surprises.

Uncle	present	watch	Grandma	visit	tea-party
letter	Cousin Alice	invitation	finally	Fido	lost
returned	unhurt				

TWO SENTENCE STORIES

Complete these sentences in any way you like and add another sentence.

1. Frank and Fred decided to go camping so they . . .
2. When the clock struck midnight in the ancient mansion . . .
3. Jack struggled on along the ledge on the cliff until . . .
4. The silence of the night was broken . . .
5. The journey along the banks of the Congo was very dangerous because of . . .
6. When the champion sprinter seemed to have the race within his grasp . . .
7. What looked like harmless logs floating in the jungle river . . .
8. Roger was usually sensible, but when he saw the ladder . . .
9. The captured soldier, tied hand and foot, did not manage to escape until . . .
10. Since the beginning of time boys have tried . . .
11. Before going to a dance girls usually . . .
12. After hours of playing football boys usually . . .

MAKING A STORY

Here are the first sentences of some short stories. Finish each story in any way you like.

1. The two teams lined up for the Cup Final.
2. The crowds were collecting for the big match.
3. Hundreds of people went to see Ringland's Circus.
4. Last week I played ice-hockey for my club.
5. Strange things happened on our first night at camp.
6. I was very nervous when I first went on stage.
7. Robinson Crusoe saw a large footprint in the sand.
8. I was bird-watching on a mountain ledge when the fog came.
9. The sledge gathered speed and Don felt afraid.
10. Tom was fishing quietly near the old oak tree.

WRITING IN PARAGRAPHS

You can tell a short story in one paragraph, or you can tell it in three or four paragraphs. A paragraph is a group of sentences dealing with one topic or idea or subject. Always begin with a 'topic' sentence. This shows what the paragraph is about.

Here is a 'topic' sentence:
Mrs. Kennedy lives by herself but she is never alone.

Here are some words to use in making a paragraph about Mrs. Kennedy:

neighbours	friends	helpful	visitors	callers	postman	social worker	doctor

Willy Grant is eleven years old. He wrote this paragraph about Mrs. Kennedy:

Granny Kennedy lives by herself but she is never alone. She lives by herself because her children are grown up. She is never lonely because she has plenty of friends and kindly neighbours. They are all very helpful. She has many visitors, such as the postman, the social worker and the doctor. The postman not only delivers her letters, he often comes in to talk to her. Mrs. Kennedy lives a happy life.

A second paragraph might deal with Granny Kennedy's view from her window. Here is a 'topic' sentence: There are lots of people in the street. Very often they visit the old lady.

Use some of these words and phrases, and others of your own, to complete this paragraph:

busy street   cars   lorries   people   babies   prams   flowers in gardens
Garrick's Grocer's Shop   Church   end of street   street corner   cats   dogs

Write a third paragraph to show that while she lives alone she has plenty to do at home.

Use the 'topic' sentence, and the words, to complete this paragraph and finish your account of Granny Kennedy:

Knitting is a useful way of passing the time.

grandson   grand-daughter   bed socks   caps   baking   cakes   bread   biscuits
home-made   radio   listening   Family Favourites   time passes quickly   busy
and contented.

SENTENCES AND PARAGRAPHS

A   Complete these sentences in any way you please:

1. I started to laugh when . . .
2. When the firing stopped . . .
3. Without stopping to think I . . .
4. Until it was daylight I could not . . .
5. Never before had I felt so foolish, all because . . .
6. The time I was most terrified was after . . .
7. Before you could say 'Jack Robinson' the vicious . . .
8. Shortly before midnight I again heard . . .
9. Although I am no coward, I really felt nervous as . . .
10. During the violent storm the climbers . . .

B   Complete the second sentences and add one or two to make paragraphs:

1. Some hobbies keep you very busy. My own hobby . . .
2. Mountain climbing can be very dangerous. I remember . . .
3. Some tramps are very interesting people. I once met . . .
4. Children should receive enough pocket money. Last week . . .
5. I have always lived in the town. I would like, however, . . .
6. Most people can be very interesting. The strangest person I have ever met . . .
7. Many wild animals are kept in cages. I do not think . . .
8. Outdoor games are better than indoor games. The reason for this is . . .
9. Travelling by ship is more enjoyable than travelling by train. Trains . . .
10. The most interesting creatures at the zoo are monkeys. Monkeys . . .

HEADLINE STORIES

A   Look at these headlines. Write an interesting paragraph on each.

1. Girl Missing from Home
2. Six Houses Flooded
3. Schoolboy Wins Bravery Medal
4. Elephant Forgets
5. Crew Feared Lost
6. World's Oldest Man
7. A Prize for Lucy
8. Tiny Tot Tricks Teacher
9. Riot at Pop Festival
10. Bargain of the Year

B   Say what these are:

1. A level crossing
2. A one-way street
3. A parking meter
4. A zebra crossing
5. A dual carriageway
6. A motorway
7. A U-turn
8. The speed limit
9. A traffic jam
10. A side street

C   Say what the difference is between the following:

1. A highwayman and a pirate
2. An employer and an employee
3. A warder and a policeman
4. A referee and an umpire
5. An enemy and an opponent
6. A helicopter and an aeroplane
7. A river and a canal
8. A sea and a lake
9. A flock and a shoal
10. A telescope and a microscope

THE ALLANDER TIMES

A Newspaper reporters write about interesting happenings or events. Here are some headlines about serious, amusing and unusual events. Imagine you are a reporter and write a short account about each event. The first sentence is given for you.

DOG SAVES PENSIONER — Mr. Samuel Goldie, aged eighty, was sleeping soundly in his flat.

FOG ON THE MOTORWAY — Last Saturday, during the rush hour, fog covered the M1 motorway at Woburn.

BANK MANAGER VANISHES — A large sum of money is reported missing from the Allander Bank.

DUCHESS COLLAPSES AT JUMBLE SALE — Gus the gorilla just loves jumble sales.

ELEPHANT IN FISH SHOP — Elsie the elephant never forgets a face.

DARING ESCAPE — A ladder was found yesterday morning outside Fairfield Jail.

GRANDFATHER JOINS CUBS — Mr. Hardy likes to visit the Ringland Lion House.

AIR-LINER HI-JACKED — A Boeing 707 has crash-landed at Kennedy Airport.

HEIRESS KIDNAPPED — A five year old Swiss girl, Greta, is missing from her home in Geneva.

TINY TIDDLY TODDLER TOPPLES TINS — Two year old Tim Taylor knocked a trolley into a stack of bean tins.

B Now imagine you saw these events taking place. First write a 'telegram' outline, then write the story of what you did. Make an interesting headline for each.
1. A street accident involving a cyclist.
2. A little girl being rescued from a burning ship.
3. A man clinging to an upturned boat being rescued by a helicopter.
4. A boy, who snatched a woman's handbag, being caught.
5. A lost child crying at a railway station.
6. A blind man with a white stick at a crossing.
7. A boy with his head stuck between railings.
8. A horse trying to get on a bus.

HOW TO WRITE A LETTER

A **Read this letter carefully and then study the rules about letter-writing given below.**

> 38, Victoria Street,
> Bristol,
> BS3 5OL.
>
> 11th. May, 1975.
>
> Dear Uncle Joe,
>   Cousin John told me that you are not keeping well. I will come to see you next Saturday. Mum and Dad send their regards and have given me one of your favourite mystery books to bring to you.
>   I scored two goals yesterday against St. Peter's. Next Monday I'm going camping on a school field trip.
>
>   Looking forward to seeing you,
>   Love,
>   Bill.

Notice these points about the letter:

1. The writer begins by putting his own address (but not his name) in the top right-hand corner. Note how the address is written out, and where the commas and full stops are placed. The date is written below the address.

2. Notice how you address the person to whom you are writing. A comma comes after the name.

3. The main part of the letter begins just below the end of the name and starts with a capital letter.

4. Note the end of the letter, the commas after the second and third last lines and the full stop after the last line.

5. Note how the writer has divided the main part of the letter into two paragraphs. He starts a new paragraph when he wants to write about a new topic. Notice that he starts the new paragraph at the same point along the line as in the first paragraph.

6. Because the writer is writing to a close relation, he uses Love at the end of the letter. He could also have written something like Best Wishes, All the best, All my love, and so on. There are many expressions you can use to close a letter. You must choose one that suits the letter and the person to whom you are writing.

B **Imagine that you are Uncle Joe and have just received Bill's letter. How would you be feeling? Write a reply to your nephew. Remember the rules you have just learnt.**

LETTERS TO WRITE

A   Here are some occasions on which you could write letters. Remember that you may not always be writing to a relation or a close friend. Sometimes, you may be writing to a complete stranger. In such a letter you would close with Yours faithfully or Yours sincerely.

1.   Write a letter to a close friend inviting him to your birthday party. Tell him the date of the party and the time at which you will expect him.

2.   Last night, when out playing, you fell and sprained your ankle, or met with some other accident. Write a letter to your teacher telling him (or her) about your accident and say when you expect to be back at school.

3.   You need some information for a school project about animals. Your teacher gives you the name and address of the local zoo. Now write to the manager of the zoo and ask for the information you want.

4.   You have just celebrated a birthday and have received a bumper present from your grandparents. Write them a thank-you letter.

5.   You have a pen pal in Australia. Write a letter to him (or her) telling about your school - its name, where it is situated, its size, the lessons you like best, the lessons you do not like, the games you play, and the holidays you get.

6.   You have recently been to see your local football team in a very important match. Write to your cousin telling him about the match.

After you have written your letter, you must remember to address the envelope correctly. Here is how Bill addressed his letter to his Uncle Joe:

> Mr. J. McNally,
> Flat 42,
>   16, Wilton Road,
>   Bristol,
>   BS1 3TQ.

Remember that the envelope must have the correct postage stamp!
B   Practise addressing the envelopes for the letters in A.

STORY BEGINNINGS

Complete these stories. Write a second paragraph for each to tell what happens next, and a third one to end the story. Give each story a title.

1. Arthur was collecting sea shells along Bondi Beach. He noticed something bobbing up and down as the tide came in. It was a dark green bottle, with something inside it. Arthur opened the cork and pulled out . . .

2. Jenny loves the sea-side and spent last summer holiday at Margate. On her first day there she hired a pedal-boat. She was having great fun until she looked towards the shore. It seemed very far away. Jenny suddenly . . .

3. Bruno was not much of a watch dog. He was far too friendly. He liked people and used to sleep outside Jimmy's bedroom, on the landing. He was hard of hearing and would never have heard a burglar. He had, however, a very keen sense of smell, and all the family were soon to be grateful for this. Late one night Bruno awoke and started to . . .

4. "What's that you've found?" shouted Benny to Noreen as they scrambled about the underground caves. "It's only an old lamp," said Noreen, "It's ever so dirty. Give me that cloth." Benny gazed idly as she rubbed the old lamp. Suddenly his eyes nearly popped out of his head. Before them . . .

5. Jenny was looking forward to spending a week with her cousin Sadie. The train arrived late at the village station. One other passenger left the train, carrying an odd-shaped parcel. Thrusting this into Jenny's arms she hissed, "Take that . . ."

6. "So that's the Old Mill Cottage," exclaimed Dennis. "Yes," replied Garry, "It's been deserted for more than a hundred years. Let's hurry on home, it's nearly midnight." "What's that?" cried Dennis, with a tremble in his voice. From the ruins . . .